Poa annua

Poa annua

Physiology, Culture, and Control of Annual Bluegrass

J. M. Vargas, Jr., and A. J. Turgeon

WILEY

John Wiley & Sons, Inc.

Copyright © 2004 by John Wiley & Sons, Inc. All rights reserved.

Published by John Wiley & Sons, Inc., Hoboken, New Jersey

Published simultaneously in Canada

For general information on our other products and services or for technical support, please contact our Customer Care Department within the United States at (800) 762-2974, outside the United States at (317) 572-3993 or fax (317) 572-4002.

Wiley also publishes its books in a variety of electronic formats. Some content that appears in print may not be available in electronic books. For more information about Wiley products, visit our web site at www.wiley.com.

Library of Congress Cataloging-in-Publication Data:

Vargas, J. M., Jr.
    Poa annua : physiology, culture, and control of annual bluegrass /
J.M. Vargas, Jr., and A.J. Turgeon
      p. cm.
Included bibliographical references and index.
    ISBN 0-471-47268-9
  1. Annual bluegrass. 2. Annual bluegrass—control. I. Turgeon, A. J.
(Alfred J.), 1943– II. Title
    SB201.B5V37 2004
    633.2'1—dc21

                           2003009067

PRINTED IN THE UNITED STATES OF AMERICA

10 9 8 7 6 5 4 3 2 1

CONTENTS

Preface   *vii*

Acknowledgments   *ix*

CHAPTER 1
Introduction
1

CHAPTER 2
Physiology
11

CHAPTER 3
Annual Bluegrass Culture
47

CHAPTER 4
Annual Bluegrass Control
101

APPENDIX 1
Herbicides Used on Annual Bluegrass Turfs
135

APPENDIX 2
Fungicides Used on Annual Bluegrass Turfs
139

APPENDIX 3
Insecticides Used on Annual Bluegrass Turfs
143

References   *147*

Index   *155*

PREFACE

ANNUAL BLUEGRASS is a very diverse species that is found growing almost everywhere in the world. In most settings it is considered a weed; thus, what has been written in the past about annual bluegrass has dealt mainly with how to control it. This is especially true in golf course turfs, where annual bluegrass has been problematic for many years. The perception of annual bluegrass as a weed reflects the assumption that it is a weak and unreliable species, especially when subjected to severe, or even moderate, environmental stresses. But this is an oversimplification of what actually happens in cultured turfgrass communities. Often, highly evolved forms of annual bluegrass can be highly persistent and enormously competitive in mixed stands with other turfgrass species.

In this book we present annual bluegrass both as a weed and as a desirable turfgrass species. We examine the anatomy, morphology, genetics, and physiology of annual bluegrass. We go into great detail on how healthy annual bluegrass greens, tees, and fairways can be maintained. Included in this discussion are the diseases and insect pests that attack annual bluegrass, the common weeds that invade annual bluegrass turfs, and how they can be controlled chemically, culturally, and, in some cases, biologically.

Our knowledge of annual bluegrass biology and culture is far from complete. In this book we have attempted to bridge the knowledge gaps with "educated guesses," which are based on our observations as well as those of our colleagues in the golf turf industry. While we have learned much from the insights shared by these colleagues, we accept full responsibility for any errors made in attempting to present what we believe to be true about annual bluegrass. Most important, we are hopeful that our fellow scientists will do the research necessary to fill these gaps and expand our knowledge of this fascinating and complex species.

ACKNOWLEDGMENTS

T HE AUTHORS wish to acknowledge the contributions of colleagues and students who helped in the preparation of the manuscript. Special thanks to Jim Snow and colleagues from the USGA Green Section, as well as to Tom Watschke, Pete Landschoot, Andy McNitt, David Huff, Floyd Giles, Bruce Branham, Ron Calhoun, and Frank Rossi for supplying photographs, illustrations, and helpful comments.

CHAPTER 1
Introduction

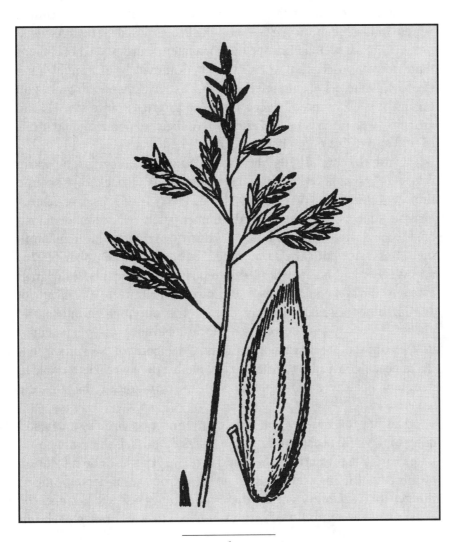

ANNUAL BLUEGRASS is the most widespread turfgrass species maintained on intensively cultured turf. It is adapted to a broad array of climatic conditions, ranging from the cold polar regions of the world to the hot deserts. Most of the top golf courses in the world have greens composed, at least in part, of annual bluegrass. The majority of the major tournaments sponsored by the United States Golf Association (USGA) and the Professional Golfers Association (PGA), as well as European tournaments, are played on greens that are composed substantially or predominantly of annual bluegrass. Despite its dominance and persistence, especially on golf greens, it is considered a weed by many turfgrass professionals and growers, and much time and energy have been expended in attempts to find and implement effective control methods.

Until the mid-1970s the loss of annual bluegrass in warm weather was believed to be due primarily to its lack of heat and drought tolerance. Then Vargas (1976, 1981, 1994) discovered that diseases such as anthracnose and summer patch were often responsible for the death of annual bluegrass during periods of high midsummer stress. At about the same time, Neimczyk and Dunbar (1976) and Wegner and Neimczyk (1981) reported that tiny black turfgrass *ataenius* and *aphodius* grubs could also contribute to the death of annual bluegrass populations during the summer months, and Tashiro et al. (1977) showed that the annual bluegrass weevil could destroy annual bluegrass populations. Once golf course superintendents began controlling these pest problems, they were better able to maintain healthy annual bluegrass turfs throughout the growing season.

Despite these developments, many turfgrass professionals still cling to the belief that summertime losses of annual bluegrass populations are due primarily to heat and drought stresses. The resolution of these conflicting views comes, in part, from an understanding of the genetic variability within the annual bluegrass species and the differential susceptibility of various biotypes to environmental condi-

ANNUAL BLUEGRASS is the most widespread turfgrass species maintained on intensively cultured turf. It is adapted to a broad array of climatic conditions, ranging from the cold polar regions of the world to the hot deserts. Most of the top golf courses in the world have greens composed, at least in part, of annual bluegrass. The majority of the major tournaments sponsored by the United States Golf Association (USGA) and the Professional Golfers Association (PGA), as well as European tournaments, are played on greens that are composed substantially or predominantly of annual bluegrass. Despite its dominance and persistence, especially on golf greens, it is considered a weed by many turfgrass professionals and growers, and much time and energy have been expended in attempts to find and implement effective control methods.

Until the mid-1970s the loss of annual bluegrass in warm weather was believed to be due primarily to its lack of heat and drought tolerance. Then Vargas (1976, 1981, 1994) discovered that diseases such as anthracnose and summer patch were often responsible for the death of annual bluegrass during periods of high midsummer stress. At about the same time, Neimczyk and Dunbar (1976) and Wegner and Neimczyk (1981) reported that tiny black turfgrass *ataenius* and *aphodius* grubs could also contribute to the death of annual bluegrass populations during the summer months, and Tashiro et al. (1977) showed that the annual bluegrass weevil could destroy annual bluegrass populations. Once golf course superintendents began controlling these pest problems, they were better able to maintain healthy annual bluegrass turfs throughout the growing season.

Despite these developments, many turfgrass professionals still cling to the belief that summertime losses of annual bluegrass populations are due primarily to heat and drought stresses. The resolution of these conflicting views comes, in part, from an understanding of the genetic variability within the annual bluegrass species and the differential susceptibility of various biotypes to environmental conditions that can threaten their survival. Rapid evolutionary development from hybridization and subsequent selection pressure can lead to new biotypes that respond differently to these conditions. Thus, a rapidly colonizing "annual" biotype that typically dies from summer heat and drought stresses after producing an abundance of seed providing a bridge to the next generation can, in time, become transformed to a slower-growing but intensely competitive "perennial" biotype that is less susceptible to these environmental stresses but which may be threatened—as are other turfgrasses—by a specific array of disease and insect pests.

In this and succeeding chapters, we clarify the roles of environmental stresses and pests in the survival and quality of annual bluegrass turfs. We begin in this chapter with a discussion of taxonomy and genetics. In Chapter 2 we focus on the physiology of annual bluegrass. In Chapter 3 we cover procedures for effectively sustaining annual bluegrass turfgrass communities. Finally, in Chapter 4, we outline procedures for effective control of annual bluegrass in mixed stands with other turfgrasses.

TAXONOMY

Annual bluegrass is a member of the *Poaceae* (formerly *Gramineae*) or grass family, *Festucoideae* (also *Pooideae*) subfamily, *Poodae* supertribe, *Festuceae* (also *Poeae*) tribe, and *Poa* genus (Chapman and Peat, 1992; Watson and Dallwitz, 1992). The genus and species (*annua*) names are usually written together as *Poa annua* to form the Latin *binomial* (Turgeon, 2002b). Often, the authority or person credited with naming the species is included in an abbreviated form (e.g., L. for Carl Linnaeus); thus, the complete Latin binomial for annual bluegrass is *Poa annua* L. In addition to annual bluegrass, common names for *Poa annua* L. include *annual meadow grass, common meadow grass, spear grass, annual spear grass, dwarf spear grass, low spear grass, six weeks grass, walk grass,* and *winter grass.*

In species in which distinct subdivisions are recognized, subspecies (ssp.), varieties (var.), forms (f.), or cultivars (cv., cultivated varieties) may be included in what is called the Latin *trinomial*. In the early literature, the term *variety* was used to distinguish plant types

differing in their respective growth habits, life lengths, and morphological features. These differences presumably reflect genetic modifications or environmental adaptations and are indicative of the
enormous variability that exists within this species. Annual biotypes
of annual bluegrass, although generally erect, are highly variable in
their morphological characteristics. As a consequence, numerous
botanical varieties have been identified and described based on such
criteria as size, shape, color, pubescence, and environmental adaptation (Table 1.1). Perennial biotypes of annual bluegrass are generally
described with long stolons that root at the nodes. As with the annual
biotypes, botanical varieties differ with respect to their morphological features (Table 1.2).

Different schemes for subdividing the annual bluegrass species
have been proposed. Tutin (1957) described four true-breeding *races*
differing in morphological features, germination, and rate of development. His characterizations include a clear differentiation between
annual and perennial biotypes. Hovin (1957b) and Youngner (1959)
also noted annual and perennial biotypes. Timm (1965) distinguished three growth types: an erect annual biotype designated ssp.
annua, a prostrate perennial biotype designated ssp. *reptans*, and a
very tall perennial biotype designated ssp. *aquatica*, which occurs on
terrestrial sites immediately adjacent to water bodies. Based on the
classical definition of a subspecies (by Stebbins, 1950: "a series of
populations having certain morphological and physiological characteristics in common, inhabiting a geographical subdivision of the
range of the species or a series of similar ecological habitats, and differing in several characteristics from typical members of other subspecies, although connected with one or more of them by a series of
integrating forms"), Gibeault and Goetze (1973) noted that between
annual and perennial biotypes:

- Significant morphological variation does exist, and length of
  life is the most obvious physiological characteristic common
  to each biotype.
- Although these biotypes do not inhabit geographic subdivisions (as they can occur in close proximity to each other),
  they do inhabit distinctly different ecological niches.

TABLE 1.1
Annual Biotypes of Annual Bluegrass (*Poa annua* L.)

Variety/Form	Description
viridis Lej. and Court.	Spikelets green with white margins on glumes and lemmas
picta Beck	Spikelets violet, 1- to 5-flowered
variegata G. Meyer	Spikelets 5- to 7-flowered; florets variegated, purple to violet
silvatica Jansen & Wachter	Spikelets exhibit silvery appearance; plants slender, small-leaved, with small inflorescences
flavescens Hausm.	Spikelets gold colored
pumila Anderss.	Spikelets 1- to 4-flowered; paleas prominently keeled; culms with 2–4 nodes and short leaves
pauciflora Fiek	Rachis 1- to 4-branched,1 spikelet/branch; spikelets 1- to 3-flowered; culms erect with small leaves
racemosa Aschers	Rachis short-branched; spikelets 1- to 3-flowered
longiglumis Lindm.	Glumes 4 to 5 mm long
latisquama Lindm.	Glumes similar to longiglumis, but ovate to semicircular
pseudopratensis Jansen & Wachter	Lower branches grouped in clusters of 4-6 (instead of being paired or solitary); branches point in all directions
bracteata (?) or *ramifers* (?)	Lower branches of inflorescence surrounded by sheath
vivipara S.F. Gray	Inflorescence viviparous (seeds germinate while still attached)
villosa Bluff and Nies	Palea with small hairs on keels; flowers small
pubescens Peterm.	Lemmas and paleas with small hairs on keels; panicles with violet variegations
rigidly Aschers	Leaves stiff, blue-green; rachis elongated; spikelets 3-flowered
macerrima Nakai ex Jansen & Wachter	Diminutive plant with small leaves and contracted inflorescences; found between bricks in walkways
umbrosa (?)	Found on shaded sites; spikelets 3- to 7-flowered
remotiflora (?)	Found in white sand in southern Europe; culms slender; plants tufted
caespitosa Terracc	Found on calcareous soils in southern Europe; leaves deep green; plants tufted, small; culms slightly compressed; panicles dense
Santiago Gay	From Chile; lemmas with three pubescent nerves

Source: Gibeault and Goetze (1973).

Introduction

TABLE 1.2
Perennial Biotypes of Annual Bluegrass (*Poa annua* L.)

Variety/Form	Description
sericea Parnell	Stems somewhat creeping; leaves short; found on wet marshy sites in Scotland
triflora Schur	Plant loosely tufted with decumbent stems extending 60 cm; leaves elongated with rounded ligules; spikelets 3- to 4-flowered; found in Europe
alpigena Schur	Culms 15–22 cm long, prostrate at base, then erect; spikelets 7- to 11-flowered; florets small, variegated; found in mountainous areas in central Europe, where it flowers in August
minima Schur	Culms 5–10 cm long; ligule short, truncate; panicle with one or two spikelets/branch; spikelets 2- to 3-flowered; lemmas green with violet variegations; found in mountainous areas in central Europe, where it flowers in July
decumbens Nolte ex Junge	Prostrate plant with long branches
nepalensis Griseb.	Stems 50 cm long; leaves 30–50 cm; panicles up to 15 cm; lemma with nerves pubescent to the middle
sikkimensis Stapf.	Leaves up to 5 mm wide; ligule 0.3–0.6 long; panicle 7.5–15 cm long; lemmas nearly glabrous; found in India
rigidiuscula L.H. Dewey	Culms 15–20 cm high with five or six nodes; leaves flat, 2–4 mm wide; ligule 2 mm long; panicle pyramidal, 3–4 cm long; spikelets 3- to 5-flowered, about 5 mm long; lemmas 3 mm long with hairs along nerves below the upper third; found (and described) in eastern Oregon; conforms to Hitchcock's (1935) description of the species
aquatica Aschers.	Culms slender, up to 50 cm tall; inflorescence large with distant spikelets; found at water's edge and on ditch banks, usually on shaded sites in central Europe

Source: Gibeault and Goetze (1973).

■ Although self-pollination within biotypes promotes stability, a small amount of cross-pollination is assumed to occur naturally, resulting in intermediate forms.

Therefore, they concluded that the three subspecies proposed by Timm should be designated *Poa annua* L. ssp. *annua* Timm, *Poa annua* L. ssp. *reptans* (Hauskins) Timm, and *Poa annua* L. ssp. *aquatica* (Aschers.) Timm. However, Warwick (1979), perhaps reflecting a more widely held view, concluded that the annual and perennial biotypes did not represent good subspecies, as they are not geographically isolated but exhibit different proportions in any given population. Currently, the annual biotype of annual bluegrass is still referred to as *Poa annua* L. var. *annua* Timm, or simply as *Poa annua* L., while the perennial biotype was designated *Poa annua* L. var. Hauskins, then redesignated *Poa annua* L. f. *reptans* (Hauskins) T. Koyama (GRIN, 1996).

GENETICS

Genetics deals with the science of inheritance, and the gene is the unit of inheritance (Lewis, 1994). Several thousand genes, each a sequence of nucleic acids forming a segment of DNA, occur linearly along a chromosome. In diploids, there are two copies of each gene positioned along homologous (i.e., structurally and sequentially similar) pairs of chromosomes. One of the copies is passed by the parent to a gamete (egg or sperm cell), which therefore contains one copy of each gene of the organism: the haploid set. When gametes from their respective parents unite to form a zygote (fertilized egg), the two haploid sets of chromosomes join to form homologous pairs containing one set of genes from paternal origin and one from maternal origin in the new diploid organism. A complete set of chromosomes, the n number, is known as a *genome*. The haploid set of chromosomes is represented as x. The letter n designates the number of chromosomes in gametophytic (i.e., sex) cells and $2n$ the chromosome number in sporophytic (vegetative) cells. For a diploid species containing 14 chromosomes, $2n = 2x = 14$. A tetraploid species has four haploid sets of chromosomes ($2n = 4x$). *Autotetraploids* contain four copies of the same genome, while *allo*tetraploids contain two copies each of two different genomes, presumably originating from very different parents.

Annual bluegrass is typically characterized as an allotetraploid species with 28 chromosomes ($2n = 4x = 28$) and is believed to have originated from a natural cross between two diploid species, each with 14 chromosomes ($2n = 2x = 14$). Nannfeldt (1937) proposed the diploids: *Poa infirma* H.B.K., an annual species, and *P. supina* Schrad., a creeping perennial, as the parent species for the initial production of *P. annua* L.; however, as he did not succeed in crossing these species by open pollination, he could not provide conclusive evidence in support of this hypothesis. Where such interspecific hybridization actually occurs, the resulting hybrid also has 14 chromosomes; however, because of the genomic differences between the parents, the resulting hybrid ($1n = 2x = 14$) is a sterile dihaploid with two sets of nonhomologous chromosomes (Figure 1.1). Hovin (1958a) concluded from studies of meioic chromosome pairing in dihaploid *P. annua* that varying levels of genome affinity exist between the parent diploid species, depending on ambient temperatures at the time of pollination. Tutin (1952) attempted to pollinate *P. annua* with pollen from *P. infirma* and produced four seeds, one of which germinated to produce a sterile hybrid that had characteristics intermediate between the two parents. As expected, the resulting triploid hybrid had 21 chromosomes: 14 from the tetraploid parent and 7 from the diploid parent. He concluded that the chromosome set from *P. infirma* must be homologous with one of the *Poa annua* sets, which could occur only if *P. infirma* were one of the parents of *P. annua*. Based on studies of chromosome structure, however, Koshy (1968) concluded that unless structural modifications of the chromosomes of *P. supina* or *P. infirma* occurred since initial hybridization, *P. annua* could not have originated from these two species; rather, it might have originated from either *P. supina* or *P. infirma* and some other unidentified diploid species. Regardless of the identity of the two parents of *P. annua*, it does appear that they were both diploids and that the result of interspecific hybridization was a sterile dihaploid, which was subsequently converted to the allotetraploid by spontaneous chromosome doubling ($2n = 4x = 28$), as shown in Figure 1.1 (Huff, 1999). The enormous variability that exists within this species is

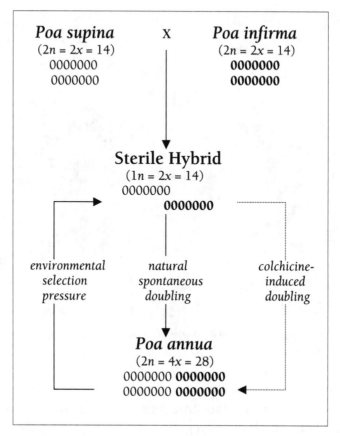

FIGURE 1.1 ■ *Proposed hybridization of* Poa *species leading to the initial formation of tetraploid* Poa annua. *(From Huff, 1999.)*

probably the result of such hybridization and doubling events. After each generation of self-pollination, however, the level of variability is reduced by half, so that eventually, strains can develop that are uniform, stable, and true breeding.

Some populations of annual bluegrass in greens have been found to be sterile dihaploids ($1n = 2x = 14$). These plants contain only half the amount of DNA (14 versus 28 chromosomes) and are more diminutive, forming very dense populations adapted to very close mowing (Figure 1.2). Huff (1999) stated that these populations provide evidence of "reverse evolution" stimulated by intense selection pressures of the golf-green environment. He hypothesized that with

FIGURE 1.2 ■ *Comparison of dihaploid (left) and tetraploid (right) annual bluegrass plants. (From Johnson et al., 1993.)*

colchicine-induced chromosome doubling, fertile plants can be developed for use in breeding programs to produce superior cultivars of annual bluegrass for use on greens and other intensively cultured turfs.

CHAPTER 2
Physiology

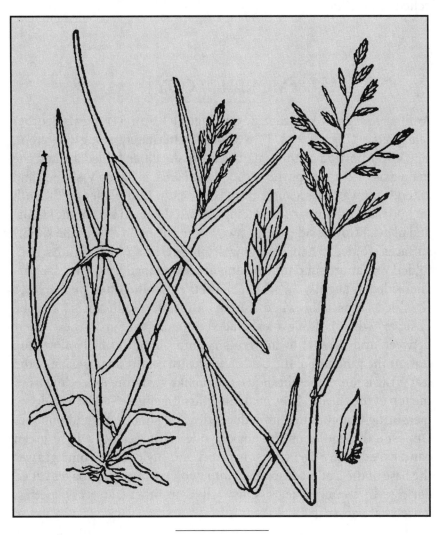

P HYSIOLOGY IS the science that deals broadly with plant forms and functions. For our purposes, it will encompass not only anatomy and morphology (forms), and growth and development (functions), but also some aspects of ecophysiology, collectively called *competition.*

MORPHOLOGY

Annual bluegrass has the morphological features typical of other bluegrasses (Figure 2.1). Leaves occur alternately along the shoot. The lower portion of the leaf, called the *sheath*, is folded around the main axis; the upper portion, called the *blade*, is flat or V-shaped and extends outward at an angle from the sheath. Leaf blades are smooth on both *adaxial* (upper side, facing toward the main axis of the shoot) and *abaxial* (lower side, facing away from the main axis of the shoot) surfaces, folded when emerging from enclosing leaf sheaths (i.e., folded vernation), and terminating in boat-shaped tips. They are parallel-sided or slightly tapering toward the tips and often puckered or wrinkled, especially when young. Multiple "light lines" can be observed when holding a leaf blade up to a light source; these occur between and parallel to the veins running longitudinally along the leaf. At the junction of the blade and sheath on the adaxial side of the leaf is the ligule, a membranous, tonguelike structure extending from the top of the sheath. In annual bluegrass, the ligule is relatively long, measuring from 0.8 to 3 mm, depending on shoot size, and pointed. Opposite the ligule, on the abaxial side of the leaf, is a light green band called the *collar*, which is broad and divided. In some grasses the base of the leaf blade extends into two clawlike appendages called *auricles.* In annual bluegrass, as well as in other bluegrass species, auricles are absent.

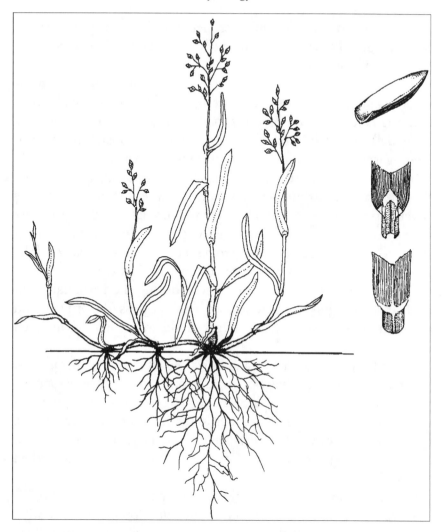

FIGURE 2.1 ■ *Morphological features of an annual bluegrass plant with close-ups (from top to bottom) of a boat-shaped leaf tip and membranous ligule on the adaxial leaf, and broad collar on the abaxial leaf, at the junction of the blade and sheath.*

At the base of the leaves and hidden within the enclosing leaf sheath is the crown. In the vegetative stage of growth, the crown is a highly compressed stem with a succession of nodes separated by very short internodes. Elongation of the internodes occurs during flowering, which signals a transition from vegetative to reproductive growth and development. A flowering culm emerges from within the enclosing leaf sheaths and terminates in an inflorescence. In annual bluegrass the panicle-type inflorescence is made up of spikelets typically composed of from three to six florets that, upon maturity, can germinate to form new plants.

There are two types of root systems present in young populations of annual bluegrass; these are the primary (or seminal) roots that originate from the embryo at germination and the adventitious (or nodal) roots that initiate from stem nodes and push through subtending leaves and into the soil. In turfgrasses, primary roots usually do not persist for more than about six months following germination; thus, in mature turfgrass communities, the entire root system is adventitious. In those annual bluegrass populations that originate from seed each year, however, primary roots can be expected to constitute a significant portion of the root system. Since elongation of the mesocotyl, an embryonic stem separating the first true leaves from the rest of the embryo, does not occur during the germination of cool-season turfgrasses, including annual bluegrass, the primary and adventitious root systems are largely indistinguishable from each other.

In addition to the crown and flowering clum, stems that may be found in some annual bluegrass populations include those associated with stolons. Stolons are lateral shoots that can grow along the surface of the ground for some distance, sometimes rooting at the nodes, before turning upward. Other lateral shoots that occur in both bunch-type and stoloniferous biotypes of annual bluegrass are called *tillers*.

In describing annual bluegrass, Sprague and Burton (1937) observed that, although occasional plants develop prostrate rooting shoots, they are not truly stoloniferous. In England, Tutin (1957) observed considerable morphological variability within annual bluegrass, including upright-growing types with light green leaves and darker low-growing types that root at the nodes of decumbent shoots. In examining plants obtained from various locations in the United States and abroad, Hovin (1957b) discovered that compared with the upright-growing, relatively short-lived types of annual bluegrass, which he classified as *annuals,* the spreading, stoloniferous types, classified as *perennials,* produced more tillers per plant, contributing to the formation of denser turfs. Youngner (1959) also recognized two general types of annual bluegrass, adding that perennials are likely to be found in greens, often forming distinct patches, while annuals are typically found in open fields and meadows. In a survey of annual bluegrass types in Europe, Timm (1965) identified three types: a decumbent vigorous perennial type, mainly from Germany; a decumbent, less vigorous, perennial type from northern Europe and the mountains of southern Europe; and an erect annual type from the Mediterranean regions.

Gibeault (1971) collected annual bluegrasses from long-established turfgrass sites at 32 locations in the U.S. Pacific Northwest. All sites were grouped into three climatic regions: coastal region I, with cool to moderate temperatures throughout the year and with most rainfall occurring during the winter months; interior region II, with cool to moderate winters and moderate to warm summer temperatures with most rainfall occurring during the summer months; and interior region III, with cool to cold winters and warm to hot summer temperatures and low annual precipitation. Most sites from which plants were collected included intensively irrigated greens, moderately irrigated fairways, and unirrigated roughs. The plants were classified as annual or perennial types based on a series of morphological characteristics, including numbers of culm nodes, secondary tillers, and adventitious roots, as well as seed dormancy and growth habit (Table 2.1). Gibeault (1971) found that annual and perennial types

TABLE 2.1

Morphological Characteristics Distinguishing Annual Bluegrass Subspecies

Morphological Characteristic	Subspecies	
	Annual	Perennial
Number of culm nodes	6 or less	7 or more
Number of secondary tillers	1 or less	2 or more
Number of adventitious roots	1 or less	2 or more
Seed dormancy	Germination 10% or less	Germination more than 10%
Growth habit	Upright	Prostrate

Source: Gibeault (1971).

of annual bluegrass were distributed equally within the three regions. Within the three management regimens, however, the distribution of types varied, depending on management and region. Greens in regions I and II contained predominantly perennial types, while in region III they included both types. In contrast, roughs were predominantly annual types in all regions; and both annual and perennial types were represented in fairways and comparably managed turfs. Gibeault concluded that the predominance of annual types in unirrigated roughs could be attributed to the lack of summer precipitation, resulting in population death and, with the resumption of favorable growing conditions in the fall, the repopulation of these sites from germinating seeds. If nondormant seeds from perennial plants germinated in response to sporadic summer precipitation, they would probably die during subsequent periods of moisture stress. This would result in selection pressure against perennial types, favoring the annual types. Conversely, on greens the perennial types would be favored where, due to frequent irrigation, moisture was not limiting. Germination of some nondormant seeds from perennial types during the summer months would favor their growth and survival, while seeds produced by annual types remained dormant and thus could not compete. Finally, in fairways the distribution of annual and perennial types would largely reflect the intensity and frequency of irrigation and perhaps other factors favoring the persistence of plants during periods of severe heat and drought stress.

ANATOMY

Bluegrass leaves have a large central vein, called a *midrib*, that separates the leaf longitudinally into two equal halves. Bulliform cells are located on either side of the central vein on the adaxial surface. Under conditions of moisture stress, these cells lose turgidity, causing the leaf to fold. This is a drought-avoidance mechanism by which the plant attempts to conserve moisture. Because of the large midrib, the abaxial surface is slightly keeled. Additional veins running parallel to the midrib occur on both sides of the leaf. Together with the central vein, these constitute the extension of the vascular system through which water, nutrients, photoassimilates, and other substances, including phytohormones, are transported throughout the plant. Surrounding the veins are loosely arranged mesophyll cells, which are completely enclosed within a single layer of epidermal cells. The mesophyll cells occupy much of the internal volume of the leaf and contain numerous chloroplasts to support photosynthetic fixation of atmospheric CO_2. Sclerotic tissue, composed of sclerenchyma cells formed by the deposition of lignin in the cell walls, typically occurs at the keel, just below the epidermis above and below the veins, and along the leaf margins. The lower density of the leaves between the veins where the mesophyll cells predominate accounts for the light lines referred to earlier. Short, stiff outgrowths of epidermal cells, called *asperites*, are sometimes evident. Cuticles vary from thin to very thin. In annual bluegrass epidermal cells are not enlarged, cuticles are very thin, and there are no asperites (Figure 2.2). Compared with Kentucky and Canada bluegrasses, annual bluegrass contains relatively little sclerotic tissue. This is consistent with results obtained by Van Arendonk and Poorter (1994), who in measuring specific leaf mass (SLM, the leaf weight per unit leaf area) in 14

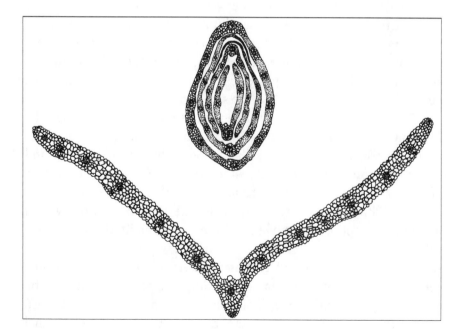

FIGURE 2.2 ▦ *Cross sections of a leaf blade (bottom) and a series of subtending leaf sheaths (top) of an annual bluegrass plant.*

turfgrasses determined that the slower-growing species with high SLM values contained more lignin and hemicellulose, while the faster-growing species with low SLM values, including annual bluegrass, contained more minerals and organic-nitrogen compounds.

Leaves arise from a growing point situated atop a stem, and they remain connected to the stem through their respective nodes for the duration of their lives. As root-absorbed water and nutrients move through a stem enroute to the leaves, the vascular system of the leaves and roots extends into and through the stems. The vascular system is organized into a series of distinct bundles surrounded by bundle sheath cells. Contained within each bundle are several large- and medium-sized xylem ducts and a series of smaller phloem ducts. The vascular bundles are separated by thin-walled parenchyma cells and are arranged in concentric rings around the outer portions of the stems. The central core of the stem in annual bluegrass is hollow. As individual vascular bundles extend basipetally through a succession of nodes along the stem they consolidate with other bundles at the nodes by a process called *anastomosis*. Vascular branches pass from the stem to axillary buds, and between the stem and adventitious roots. Cross-linking of vascular bundles provides for assimilate movement across the stem and between leaves. Vascular branches entering an axillary bud are derived both from the subtending leaf and from bundles on the opposite side of the stem, connecting the bud to leaves above and below the subtending node.

The vascular system in an adventitious root extends through the root's inner core, called the *stele*. Most of the remaining volume of the root is made up of cortex cells bordered by the epidermis and endodermis on the outside and inside, respectively. The inner surface of the transverse and radial primary walls of the endodermal cells exhibits a band of suberin, known as the *Casparian strip*, which impedes the apoplastic movement (i.e., movement through intercellular spaces or through pores within cell walls) of water and dissolved materials into the stele. Water is diverted into the endodermal cells following an osmotic gradient through the pericycle and into the conducting cells of the xylem. Movement of dissolved materials also must take place through the membranes of the living endodermal cells and therefore depends on energy from respiration. Where turfgrasses are growing in severely compacted or waterlogged soils, oxygen for root respiration may be so deficient that transport of materials within the roots is restricted. This condition can result in wet wilt and other adverse effects commonly observed in turfgrasses.

As the stele's xylem vessels are continuous with those within the vascular bundles distributed through the stems and leaves, water can move readily to the leaves through continuous unobstructed channels. The force that pulls water through these vascular channels is *transpiration*. This is the evaporation of moisture from inside the leaf and the subsequent movement of accumulated water vapor into the atmosphere through stomatal openings in the leaf epidermis (Figure 2.3). The evaporative process occurs primarily from water films surrounding the mesophyll cells. As these moisture films become smaller, a water potential gradient is established between the mesophyll cells and the vascular bundles, or veins, causing water from the xylem vessels to diffuse across the leaf to replenish water lost from transpiration. Stomatal openings not only allow water vapor to exit the leaf, but permit the exchange of O_2 and CO_2 between the leaf and the atmosphere outside. Since CO_2 is consumed and O_2 produced through photosynthesis, such exchanges across stomatal openings are essential for healthy plant growth. The photoassimilates

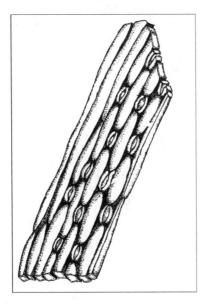

FIGURE 2.3 ■ *Upper (adaxial) surface of an annual bluegrass leaf blade showing epidermal cells and guard cells with open stomates.*

resulting from initial fixation of atmospheric CO_2 are distributed to other parts of the plant through continuous phloem ducts contained within the vascular system.

GERMINATION AND SEEDLING DEVELOPMENT

A *floret* (Figure 2.4) is composed of a caryopsis sandwiched between two floral bracts, called the *palea* and the *lemma*. The concave surface of the palea, along with the margins of the subtending lemma, are evident on the adaxial side of the floret. At the base of the palea is the *rachilla,* a short clublike structure extending upward and outward. The convex surface of the lemma is five-nerved and pubescent along the lower portions of the nerves, and completely dominates the abaxial side of the floret. The floret's pubescence probably contributes to its success in being easily transported by shoes, implements, and other methods of conveyance (Peel, 1982; Tutin, 1957). The *caryopsis* is the "grain" of a grass plant; it contains the true seed, which is surrounded by the remnants of the ovary wall, called the

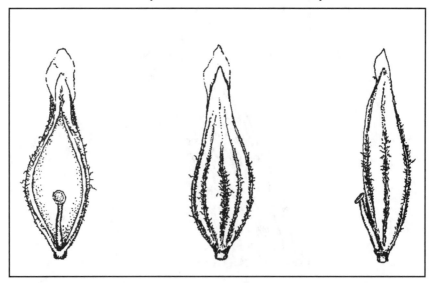

FIGURE 2.4 ■ *Mature annual bluegrass floret with palea (left), lemma (middle), and side (right) views.*

pericarp. Contained within the seed is the *embryo,* a mobile miniature plant occupying less than 20 percent of the internal volume of the seed. The *endosperm,* the food supply for sustaining the plant during germination and until it is capable of producing its own food through photosynthesis, makes up the rest of the internal volume of the seed.

The germination process begins when the seed absorbs water. This triggers the production of hydrolytic enzymes that break down the starch and proteins in the endosperm to simpler carbohydrates and amino acids for nourishing the embryo. These enzymes are actually produced in the aleurone layer, located just inside the seed coat, in response to gibberellins from the embryo. The first structural development evident during germination is the enlargement of the coleorhiza, located at the base of the embryo, and the emergence of root-hairlike structures that anchor the embryo to the soil. A *radicle,* or primary root, pushes through the side of the coleorhiza and grows into the soil (Figure 2.5). At about the same time, the *coleoptile,* a sheath of translucent tissue surrounding the growing point, emerges above the soil surface. Within the emerging coleoptile the first leaf

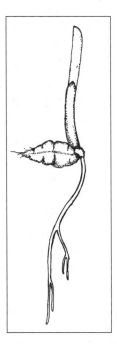

FIGURE 2.5 ■ *Annual bluegrass seedling showing a primary root emerging from the coleorhiza, and the first leaf emerging from the top of the coleoptile.*

elongates and pushes out through a pore at the tip of the coleoptile. Photosynthetic activity begins, and soon the seedling becomes entirely independent of the endosperm for its food. Subsequent leaf growth also occurs through the coleoptile and within the folds of older leaves. Eventually, the coleoptile withers away and only leaves are evident above the soil surface. The next seedling structures to form are the adventitious roots, which develop from nodes at the base of the new shoot, to complement the primary roots developed earlier.

The literature dealing with annual bluegrass seed germination is filled with apparent inconsistencies. For example, Beard (1970) observed that germination of annual bluegrass in Michigan occurs primarily during cool, moist conditions in late summer or early fall, with spring germination evident in some areas. Neidlinger (1965) concluded from his research in Oregon that since maximum temperatures under a turfgrass canopy on sunny days were within those permitting annual bluegrass germination, seeds could germinate throughout the summer in established turf. Lush (1988a) found in studies on a golf green in southeastern Australia that annual reestablishment from seed occurs in a three-month germination "pulse" beginning in late spring. Drawing from results obtained by Youngner (1959), she also suggested that fall germination may be more likely where summer droughts occur. The question then arises: Is a germination pulse primarily a reflection of temperature or moisture? Cockerham and Whitworth (1967) found that annual bluegrass germination was slightly higher at a constant temperature of 60°F (16°C) than at either 50°F (10°C) or 70°F (21°C), whereas Bogart (1972) reported no differences in germination at constant temperatures of 40°F (4°C), 50°F (10°C), 60°F (16°C), or 70°F (21°C), but a very substantial decrease at 80°F (27°C) and 90°F (32°C). Hovin (1957b) found that alternating temperatures promoted higher rates of annual bluegrass seed germination compared with constant temperatures. Engel (1967) reported that the alternating day/night temperatures of 86°/68°F (30°C/20°C) resulted in higher germination than constant temperatures of 86°F (30°C) or 68°F (20°C). Beard et al. (1978) reported consistently high germination, averaging more than 80 percent, at alternating day/night temperatures of 65°/45°F (18°C/7°C), 75°/55°F (24°C/13°C), and 85°/65°F (29°C/18°C), but a decrease to 63.5 percent at 55°/35°F (13°C/2°C). It appears from these studies that annual bluegrass germination occurs across a wide temperature range, with some reduction in percentages at very low or very high temperatures. Allen et al. (1993) studied the effects of alternating cycles of hydration and dehydration on annual bluegrass germination. Cycling generally resulted in delayed, but more uniform germination. Cycled seeds required fewer hours in contact with liquid water to germinate than did continuously hydrated seeds and were not killed by repeated dehydration for up to 24 hours at –10 MPa. They determined that annual bluegrass seeds were prevented from germinating by 8-hour hydration phases coupled with 16- to 24-hour dehydration phases at –10 MPa. Upon transfer to continuous hydration, however, seeds germinated within 36 hours. This suggests that annual bluegrass seeds can germinate successfully even with only intermittent hydration. Therefore, depending on the efficacy of a turfgrass canopy in moderating temperatures at the ground surface, some germination could be taking place throughout the growing season, provided that adequate—but not necessarily continuous—moisture is available.

Cockerham and Whitworth (1967) found that freshly harvested annual bluegrass seed from New Mexico failed to germinate; however, after aging for one and two months, germination at 60°F (16°C) was 26 and 47 percent, respectively. These results indicated a seed dormancy period. Tutin (1957) also found a dormancy period with an upright-growing annual biotype of annual bluegrass, but observed no dormancy with a perennial biotype of the same species. In California, Wu and Harivandi (1993) measured germination of annual bluegrass seed collected from golf course roughs and greens. They found that at a constant temperature of 68°F (20°C), germination of the seed from roughs was uniformly low, averaging less than 20 percent, while germination from the green was high, averaging over 80 percent. At 52°F (11°C), however, germination was uniformly high, with no distinguishable difference between green and rough populations. Clearly, the annual bluegrass populations in the roughs and greens, and the seeds obtained from them, were very different. Lush (1989) stated that nearly 100 percent of seeds collected from a golf green germinated readily, but that seeds collected from a nearby fairway and rough germinated only after they were chilled. When these seeds were used to produce a subsequent generation of seeds, germination of both chilled and unchilled seeds from the green was nearly 100 percent at all dates tested. However, germination of unchilled seeds from the fairway was 0, 24.3, and 80 percent at 3.5 to 4.5, 6.5, and 11.5 months after heading, respectively. From the rough, germination of unchilled seeds was 0, 26.3, and 78.8 percent at 3.5 to 4.5, 6.5, and 11.5 months after heading, respectively. Conversely, germination of chilled seeds from the fairway and rough was generally high at all dates. Wu et al. (1987) also found that annual bluegrass seeds from a rough were dormant until chilled, while those from a green had no chilling requirement. Other sources listed a chilling requirement for annual bluegrass germination (Bewley and Black, 1994) but did not differentiate among biotypes.

Other factors that have been reported as having an influence on annual bluegrass seed germination include light and soil pH and nutrient status. Annual bluegrass seed germination is favored by light; however, germination does occur in the absence of light, provided that other conditions are favorable (Engel, 1967; Hovin, 1957a; Neidlinger, 1965). Ferguson (1936) concluded that acid-forming fertilizers, such as ammonium sulfate, inhibited annual bluegrass germination through a reduction in pH. Cockerham and Whitworth (1967) observed increased germination, from 60 to 85 percent, when a 0.1 percent potassium nitrate solution was used in place of water to provide moisture for the germinating seeds. The germination process, beginning with absorption of water and concluding with emergence of the coleoptile, may be completed within 7 days or require several weeks (Juhren et al., 1957), depending on temperature, light intensity, photoperiod, and perhaps other conditions.

In conclusion, annual bluegrass seed germination can occur over a wide range of temperatures, provided that adequate moisture is available. Although other external factors, such as light, pH, and nutrients, may also affect germination significantly, it can still occur despite the lack of light and nutrients and across a wide range of soil pH values. Seed dormancy occurs in some (rough-type, perhaps fairway-type) annual bluegrass biotypes, presumably to inhibit germination under unfavorable summer conditions but not in other (greens-type) biotypes. Where it occurs, seed dormancy can be overcome with time and through a low-temperature (chilling) treatment.

SHOOT GROWTH

The shoot is an integration of a stem and its associated leaves and buds. In addition to aerial shoots that grow more or less vertically, some annual bluegrass biotypes also produce decumbent shoots called *stolons*. Shoots can be either vegetative or reproductive, depending on whether or not inflorescences have formed and emerged from their growing points. New shoots are always vegetative. After a period of maturation, however, some shoots become reproductive (refer to the section "Inflorescence Development" later in this chapter).

A growing point is situated atop a stem and forms leaf primordia continually when growing vegetatively. Leaf primordia arise due to cell division just below the apical meristem. Subsequent meristematic activity is restricted to the basal portion of the leaf primordium, establishing the intercalary meristem. With continued development, the intercalary meristem divides into two distinct meristems: an upper intercalary meristem that produces cells for growth of the leaf blade, and a lower intercalary meristem that remains at the base of the leaf to continue development of the leaf sheath. Following the emergence of a new leaf above the enclosing leaf sheaths, the new blade and sheath assume different shapes. The blade unfolds to form a relatively flat structure, while the sheath remains in a folded configuration surrounded by older leaf sheaths. Eventually, a turfgrass leaf undergoes senescence beginning at the tip and extending downward, and falls away from the shoot. As the number of leaves per shoot generally remains constant under a specific set of environmental conditions, the rate of new leaf emergence is approximately the same as the rate at which older leaves die. The rate at which new leaves appear varies with genotype, climatic conditions, and fertilization practices. The time interval between the appearance of successive leaves is called a *plastochron* and is usually measured in days. The shortest plastochrons occur under optimum temperatures, high light intensities, high levels of nitrogen fertilization, and optimum soil moisture conditions. Lush (1989) measured plastochrons for both annual bluegrass and creeping bentgrass of 5.5 and 6.5 days per leaf at constant temperatures of 72°F (22°C) and 90°F (32°C), respectively.

Other stems of importance in turfgrasses are those associated with stolons. These are elongated stems that arise from axillary buds on the crown. During early internode elongation the entire stem segment between nodes may be meristematically active. As the internode continues growth, cell division becomes restricted to regions directly ahead of each node, forming the stem intercalary meristems. Stolons grow along the surface of the ground and form roots at the nodes.

Like stolons, *tillers* develop from axillary buds along the crown; however, tillers differ in that they grow upward and within the sheaths of enclosing leaves, whereas stolons grow outward from the mother shoot. With profuse tillering there is a dramatic increase in the number of new shoots occurring immediately adjacent to the parent shoots. Considering the impact of tillering in conjunction with lateral growth of stolons, which also produce tillers, one can visualize how a dense stand of shoots can soon develop from a single seedling.

In an annual bluegrass population individual shoots eventually die and must be replaced by new shoots to maintain a desired density level. Turfgrasses are perennials not because individual shoots survive indefinitely, but because the plant community is dynamic, with dying members continually being replaced by new ones. The lives of individuals vary with genotypes and environmental conditions. Estimates of the longevity of perennial biotypes range from 13 to 19 months (Wells, 1975) to two to three years (Tutin, 1957); however, more recent literature suggests that it may be much broader.

Lush (1988a) observed that at a density of 174 shoots/in^2 (27 shoots/cm^2) encountered in a 14-year-old green in southeastern Australia, the life of an individual shoot was very short, lasting no more than 3 months. As the death of each shoot was matched by the birth of another, she estimated that there were four complete turnovers of shoots in the course of a calendar year. She also reported that seed numbers in the soil ranged from a low of 19 seeds/in^2 (3 seeds/cm^2) during the fall and winter months to a maximum of 135 seeds/in^2 (21 seeds/cm^2) in spring after flowering, and attributed perennial populations of annual bluegrass to overlapping generations of annual plants from seed.

Huff (1998) measured densities of some selections from 80-year-old greens in Pennsylvania that reached 1300 shoots/in^2 (200 shoots/cm^2) suggesting that over a period of many decades, annual bluegrass populations of exceptional quality can evolve in contemporary greens-type environments. Some of his selections had very little vertical shoot growth and produced few or no inflorescences. Since no viable seeds are produced in sterile populations of annual bluegrass, the sustained density and lateral spreading of these populations must be due to strictly vegetative growth, with essentially no contributions from germinating seeds.

ROOT GROWTH

The root is made up of an organized arrangement of cells produced by the division of meristematic cells located just behind the root cap. The root cap protects the root meristem from abrasion by soil particles as growth proceeds through the soil. Meristematic cells both replenish the root cap and provide for tip growth of the root itself. Following division the new cells elongate and push the root cap through the soil. Maturation and differentiation of elongated cells result in the development of specialized tissues for absorbing and transporting water and nutrients to other parts of the plant.

As discussed earlier, seminal roots develop from the embryo, while adventitious roots develop at stem nodes along stolons and from lower portions of crowns. Depending on the position of the stem from which roots emerge, they grow outward from the plant and turn downward. Lateral or branch roots begin as root initials within the pericycle inside the stele and grow through living root tissue to the outside, initially at right angles to their parent root, then downward. Recently initiated roots appear thick and white. Roots become thinner and darker with age. Root decay begins in the epidermis and cortex and eventually spreads to the stele. The cortex may slough off through a process called *decortication* in older portions of a root; however, the bare stele may still be capable of transporting water and nutrients from the region of absorption to aerial parts of the plant.

The life span of adventitious roots may be as long as that of the shoot they support; however, climatic stresses and unfavorable soil conditions may cause death of roots, while their associated shoots survive. This is most likely to occur in cool-season turfgrasses during midsummer stress periods. Most root initiation and growth of cool-season grasses occur in spring and, to a lesser extent, during cool weather in the fall. From field observations, especially on compacted and poorly drained soils, annual bluegrass has frequently been described as a shallow-rooted species (Ferguson, 1936; Goss, 1964; Madden, 1967). But Sprague and Burton (1937) proposed that the limitation of roots to the surface inch or two of soil on sites dominated by annual bluegrass is indicative of unfavorable soil conditions, not of the inability of roots to grow more deeply. In tests conducted on both compacted and loose soils, annual bluegrass dry root weights were 34.8 and 59.6 lb per 1000 ft^2 (17.0 to 29.1 kg per 100 m^2), respectively. Furthermore, within the 10-in. (25.4-cm) soil profile examined, 70 percent of the roots were within the top inch of the compacted soil, and 59 percent were in the top 1 in. (2.54 cm) of the loose soil. Also, they found no significant difference in root weights of annual bluegrass, Kentucky bluegrass, and colonial bentgrass growing in loose soils. They concluded that annual bluegrass does not inherently develop a shallow root system unless forced to do so by unfavorable soil conditions, and that root growth in severely compacted soils is largely confined to cooler seasons when the roots' oxygen requirements are lower. Wilkinson and Duff (1972) also found no difference in root growth of annual bluegrass, Kentucky bluegrass, and creeping bentgrass when grown in the same soils. They also measured decreases in root weight with increasing depth; however, the magnitude of the decreases was surprisingly small, with only 29 percent of the annual bluegrass roots contained in the top inch of soil. Comparing root growth of these species at three levels of compaction (1.1, 1.25, and 1.4 g/cm^3) in a sandy loam soil, they found that root growth of all species actually increased with increasing compaction. Based on an extensive volume of published research (Glinski and Lipiec, 1990), this direct relationship between compaction and root growth is contrary to what would have been expected. Given the soil texture and experimental methods employed, however, the highest bulk density (1.4 g/cm^3) may have been too low to affect root growth adversely. Based on studies of rooting and heat tolerance, Cordukes (1977) concluded that given good soil and growth conditions, annual bluegrass should not be characterized as intolerant of heat stress and does not rate the reputation of a shallow-rooted species. Waddington and Zimmerman (1972) found a direct relationship between water table depth and rooting depth of annual bluegrass. Again, root growth appeared to be limited by unfavorable conditions within the soil profile. Youngner (1959) suggested that the tolerance of annual bluegrass to low soil oxygen levels enhances its competitive ability in mixed communities.

INFLORESCENCE DEVELOPMENT

The grass flower develops on a rachilla and within the axil of a lemma. Immediately below the flower is the palea, which, together with the lemma, enfolds the flower. The lowermost organs of the grass flower are the two lodicules, which function in opening the floret to expose the flower at anthesis. The lodicules become turgid at a particular stage of floral maturation and force the lemma and palea to separate for the exsertion of stigmas and anthers. The male portion of the flower is composed of three stamens that consist of pollen-bearing anthers and their filaments. The female portion is the pistil, which is composed of a single ovary and two feathery stigmas and styles. At anthesis the slender filaments elongate rapidly and then shrivel up after releasing their pollen. Subsequent transfer of pollen to the stigmas is termed *pollination*.

Once a pollen grain comes into contact with the stigma a pollen tube grows through the style and into the ovule within the ovary. Upon entering the embryo sac two sperm nuclei are released. One unites with the egg to form a zygote, and the other unites with two polar nuclei to form the endosperm cell. These sexual unions involving sperm nuclei are termed *double fertilization*. The zygote or fertilized egg forms the embryo, and the fertilized endosperm cell eventually develops into the endosperm, the food source for the embryo during germination.

Formation of the grass inflorescence occurs in four distinct phases: maturation of the plant, induction of the flowering stimulus, initiation of the stem apex, and development of the flowers. Until maturation a juvenile plant is insensitive to environmental conditions that later promote flowering. During induction, physiological changes take place in the plant in response to specific environmental conditions. Two types of induction processes are known to exist: low-temperature induction, called *vernalization*, which occurs in the growing point, and photoperiodic induction, which takes place in the leaves.

The third phase of inflorescence formation is initiation. This involves the transformation of the stem apex from a vegetative to a flowering axis. The first detectible response during initiation is the rapid elongation of the stem apex. At this time leaf primordia form in rapid succession and the overall length of the stem apex is increased dramatically. The second response is the development of lateral buds in the axils of leaf primordia, resulting in the formation of double ridges along the stem apex. The fourth and final phase of inflorescence formation, called *development,* includes all the events leading to the formation of branches, spikelets, and florets, and the elevation of the inflorescence above the leaves (Figure 2.6).

FIGURE 2.6 ■ *Panicle-type inflorescence of annual bluegrass emerging from the boot.*

Once the stem apex transforms from the vegetative to the flowering state, no further leaf primordial production occurs. Therefore, removal of the inflorescence by mowing does not remove future leaf-producing structures but, rather, may stimulate the development of subsidiary tillers and thus enhance leaf production. The future destiny of the flowering shoot, however, is terminal, and perenniality in the turfgrass community depends on the growth of nonflowering shoots and new plants from intravaginal and extravaginal branching.

Annual bluegrass spikelets were described as 3- to 10-flowered by Hubbard (1959), 3- to 6-flowered by Gleason (1968), and 3- to 8-flowered by Warwick (1979). Johnson (1991) found that that the number of florets per spikelet varied among biotypes and with plant density. In low-density populations the number of florets per spikelet among six biotypes ranged from 3.1 to 4.2, while in high-density populations the range was from 2.2 to 3.5. Johnson et al. (1993) concluded that a significant genotype by environment interaction due to plant density occurred for the number of florets per spikelet and seed yield for an inflorescence. Genotypes with coarser habits are affected more by density than are finer-textured, more compact genotypes. Lush (1988a) found only one or two florets per spikelet in golf greens. Of the annual bluegrass inflorescences present in spring, 17 percent had three spikelets and 80 percent had at least two. Sarukhan (1974) found that some plants absorb the effects of increased density by reducing the number of seeds produced while maintaining the weight of individual seeds. Law (1975) initially estimated annual bluegrass seed production at 80 viable seeds per plant when growing in low-density populations. Later, Law et al. (1977) determined that seed number per inflorescence varied depending on shoot density, season, and the particular genotype selected. Disarticulation (separation) of the spikelet at maturity occurs above the glumes and frequently between florets in annual bluegrass.

Although annual bluegrass has been observed to flower all through the growing season, distinct pulses of flowering are often observed. The main flowering period in North America and northern Europe occurs in late spring and in summer (Beard et al., 1978; Gibeault, 1974; Law, 1981; Wells, 1974); whereas in southeastern Australia, the flowering pulse reaches its peak in early to midspring (Lush, 1988a). Annual bluegrass seedhead production occurred only after soil temperatures surpassed 59°F (15°C) (Bogart, 1972). Danneberger and Vargas (1984) demonstrated the usefulness of degree-day accumulation for predicting seed head emergence. They found that maximum seed head production occurred for a period of 14 to 18 days; however, the peak occurred on May 21 in 1982 and on June 3 in 1983. Degree-days were calculated, beginning April 1, by adding the daily maximum and minimum temperatures, dividing by 2 to calculate the average temperature, then subtracting the baseline temperature of 55°F (13°C). Where positive values were achieved, the daily degree-days were recorded and accumulated over time. The peak in seed head production occurred at 363 to 433 degree-days. They concluded that calculating degree-days provides a more reliable estimate of seed head emergence than simply following the calendar.

Juhren et al. (1957) found that flowering was earlier and more abundant with cool temperatures and short photoperiods. Johnson and White (1997a) stated that whereas the true annual biotypes were day-neutral and photoperiod insensitive, some perennial and intermediate biotypes were sensitive to long-day conditions whereas others required cold treatment or short days to flower. They concluded that photoperiodism is associated with perenniality and may be important in allocations between vegetative and reproductive growth , as well as variation and adaptability of the species. Johnson and White (1997b) found that vernalization (cold-temperature treatment that induces a vegetative meristem to become reproductive) in many perennial biotypes synchronizes flowering to the spring season and promotes vegetative growth (i.e., prevents flowering) for the remainder of the year; however, they encountered perennial biotypes with continuous flowering during the summer. The annual biotype was not sensitive to vernalization treatments (and was day neutral), whereas all perennial biotypes were (i.e., vernalization—not photoperiod—was the primary floral-induction mechanism); however, each of these differed with respect to length of juvenile period, length of vernalization exposure, vernalization temperature, and number of inflorescences per stolon. These differing requirements influence reproduction timing and may explain the diversity within the annual bluegrass species. Selection for longer cold-treatment requirements and less induction in short days may reduce the amount of flowering exhibited in the stand.

Physiology

Annual bluegrass possesses the remarkable ability to ripen viable seeds on panicles excised from the plant on the same day that pollination occurs, contributing to its success in turfgrass and other plant communities (Koshy, 1969). Ruemmele (1989) found that the time between stigma exertion from female (male sterile) florets to dehiscence of the anthers on the nearest perfect (hermaphroditic) florets ranged from 1 hour to more than 1 day. Law (1979) initially estimated annual bluegrass seed production at 80 viable seeds per plant when growing in low-density populations.

Comparisons of erect and prostrate types of annual bluegrass revealed that the erect type flowered sooner and had higher seed production (Law et al., 1977). While resulting in more progeny for future generations, the diversion of resources to reproduction and away from other essential activities, such as maintenance and growth, leads to increased risk of mortality and reduced potential for reproduction later in the life of the individual (Law, 1979). Warwick and Briggs (1978a) found that erect and prostrate types flower 55 and 80 days, respectively, after sowing and concluded that growth form and flowering behavior were determined genetically and that the predominance of prostrate individuals in greens might be a selective advantage under conditions of repeated close mowing.

Johnson et al. (1993) observed that annual biotypes of annual bluegrass often flower continually throughout the growing season and thus termed them *continual* types, whereas those flowering only in spring (and occasionally in fall) were termed *seasonal* types; however, some perennial biotypes exhibit continual flowering and might be considered intermediate between annual and perennial biotypes.

Tutin (1957) concluded that annual bluegrass is primarily self-pollinated. He attributed this to limited pollen dispersal under calm conditions, due to the production of large heavy pollen and the close position of the inflorescences to the ground. Johnson et al. (1993) also proposed that self-pollination is favored due to early pollen shed (between 3:00 and 8:00 A.M.) on compact inflorescences, especially under high-density conditions. In contrast, Koshy (1969) characterized annual bluegrass as either self- or cross-pollinated, based on an efficient mechanism of pollen liberation with stigma exsertion, which promotes cross-pollination and a high degree of self-incompatibility. Examination of unopened florets revealed that pollen liberation in the closed floret, called *cleistoamy,* does not occur, and as a consequence, self- and cross-pollination are equally likely. He also presented evidence that apomixis does not operate in annual bluegrass. Ellis (1973) examined populations of annual bluegrass from Wales and Australia and found low percentages of verifiable hybridization, ranging from 0 to 7.22 percent, indicating that reproduction is sexual and largely inbreeding; however, he acknowledged that some hybrids are difficult to identify, due to the similarity of characteristics used for differentiating the parent plants. He proposed that outcrossing could actually vary from 0 to 15 percent, depending on wind, rain, and other environmental conditions, as well as population size. He concluded that self-pollination would be advantageous to a colonizing species such as annual bluegrass, as genetic stability, maintained by inbreeding, would be most important during the dispersal and establishment phases of colonization, when success depends on the preadaptation of the genotypes. Subsequent expansion, however, would be facilitated by the ability to extend the range of variation of the population by recombination through a low level of outcrossing. Darmency and Gasquez (1983) showed that outcrossing could range from 1 to 22 percent at high plant densities. As both erect and prostrate growth variants have similar gene frequencies and similar frequencies of heterozygotes, natural hybridization is likely.

Another factor that may account for the extent that outcrossing occurs is temperature. A day/night temperature regimen of 82°F/68°F (28°C/20°C) caused emerging panicles to have either shriveled anthers with nonfunctional pollen or no anthers, while the pistillate organs were fully functional (Hovin, 1957b, 1958b). As a consequence, nearly all of the resulting seeds were F_1 hybrids. Shriveled stamens and nonfunctional pollen were not observed, however, where a lower (73°F, 23°C constant) temperature was employed (Koshy, 1969).

Johnson et al. (1993) concluded that the intensively cultured environment of a green seems to favor selfing behavior and that this demonstrates an efficient survival strategy. Although most grass flowers begin to shed pollen after the inflorescence has been largely extended from the restrictive boot, in many annual bluegrasses (especially perennial dwarf types), anthesis often begins when only two or three spikelets have emerged (Johnson and White, 1998).

Since this flowering habit would not exchange pollen between plants, it is likely that these genotypes are almost exclusively selfing in nature and thus would tend to breed true to type. The more annual biotypes extend more fully before anthesis, allowing the inflorescence to be more open to airborne pollen, thus favoring cross-pollination. In between selfing and crossing is *sibbing*; this refers to pollination between florets on different but genetically related plants within a population. This can be described by the inbreeding coefficient (F). In selfing or inbreeding, F = 1, as there is no variation introduced via pollination and subsequent fertilization. Where outcrossing occurs between genetically different plants, F = 0, as there is considerable exchange of genetic information between male and female parents and considerable variation introduced in the offspring. In sibbing, the inbreeding coefficient will be somewhere between 0 and 1 (0 < F < 1), depending on the magnitude of genetic differences existing between male and female parents.

Allard et al. (1968) predicted that variation in a population is likely to be maintained when outcrossing percentages as low as 5 percent occur; therefore, the low rate of outcrossing presumed to occur in most annual bluegrass populations would be adequate to maintain the ability to adapt to changing environmental conditions, called *plasticity*, often observed in this species. In investigations conducted by Darmency et al. (1992), erect and prostrate populations of annual bluegrass from France and Switzerland were allowed to cross-pollinate; hybrids between variants were identified by their heterozygosity (AB) at the *Est 1* locus. These were then allowed to self-pollinate to produce the F_2 generation. Flowering time and tiller length were the only characteristics consistently separating the two growth variants, whereas the hybrids were typically intermediate in value. The parental associations of leaf length and width, and flowering time and tiller length, were maintained, suggesting linkage of major genes for these traits, whereas other associations, such as flowering time and tiller number, and leaf length and tiller number and length, were not.

Johnson et al. (1993) proposed that the control of flowering habit fits a single-locus, two-allele model, with continual flowering completely dominant. With single-gene control of the characteristic, outcrossing to another population could result in dramatic changes in plant form. Sweeney and Danneberger (1997) proposed a process by which gene flow—movement of pollen from one population to another, or movement of seed from one area to another—might occur within and between highly differentiated annual bluegrass populations in greens and adjacent fairways. They illustrated this with an example in which all surviving annual bluegrass in the green came from nondormant seed and thus had both recessive alleles (*dd*) for nondormancy, while all of the annual bluegrass in the fairway had either both alleles for dormancy (*DD*) or one allele for dormancy and one for nondormancy (*Dd*). If the *Dd* genes constituted 90 percent of the fairway population, the seed produced within the fairway would have 35 percent *DD*, 45 percent *Dd*, and 20 percent *dd*; therefore, 20 percent of the seed would be nondormant, despite the fact that none of the parents came from nondormant seed (Table 2.2). If the annual bluegrass in the green were entirely self-pollinated, all seed produced would be dormant (i.e., carrying only *dd* alleles); however, if the annual bluegrass in the green were pollinated entirely by the annual bluegrass in the fairway, the seed produced would have 55 percent *Dd* genes and thus would be dormant, while 45 percent would have *dd* genes and would be nondormant (Table 2.3). This illustrates the tremendous opportunities that exist for genetic recombination within and between annual bluegrass populations. With selection pressures operating on the new populations resulting from these seed, annual bluegrass can undergo dramatic evolutionary changes over relatively short periods of time. Because dormancy influences the competitive relationship between different plant populations in specific environments, Sweeney and Danneberger (1995, 1997) chose a trait to study the amount of genetic interaction between greens and fairways that did not have this effect; specifically, they chose to look at differences in RAPD markers, which show differences in small portions of DNA. Pieces of DNA are paired with short sequences of complementary RNA, called *primers*, and amplified (i.e., copied more than 1 million times) so that the resulting fluorescent DNA can be seen under ultraviolet light. DNA that isn't complementary to the primers isn't amplified and is undetectable. The presence or absence of a fluorescing band following gel separation represents genetic differences. Based on the findings of no difference among greens—but detectable differences within and among fair-

TABLE 2.2

Distribution of Gametes for Dormancy (*D*) and Nondormancy (*d*) among Annual Bluegrass Populations in a Fairway Producing Entirely Dormant Seed in Which 90 Percent of the Plants Contain the Recessive (*d*) Allele[a]

		Male Fairway Parent									
		DD	Dd	Dd	Dd	Dd	Dd	Dd	Dd	Dd	Dd
	DD	DD DD DD DD	DD DD DD Dd	DD DD DD Dd	DD DD DD Dd	DD DD DD Dd	DD DD DD Dd	DD DD DD Dd	DD DD DD Dd	DD DD DD Dd	DD DD DD Dd
	Dd	DD DD DD Dd	DD Dd Dd dd	DD Dd Dd dd	DD Dd Dd dd	DD Dd Dd dd	DD Dd Dd dd	DD Dd Dd dd	DD Dd Dd dd	DD Dd Dd dd	DD Dd Dd dd
	Dd	DD DD DD Dd	DD Dd Dd dd	DD Dd Dd dd	DD Dd Dd dd	DD Dd Dd dd	DD Dd Dd dd	DD Dd Dd dd	DD Dd Dd dd	DD Dd Dd dd	DD Dd Dd dd
	Dd	DD DD DD Dd	DD Dd Dd dd	DD Dd Dd dd	DD Dd Dd dd	DD Dd Dd dd	DD Dd Dd dd	DD Dd Dd dd	DD Dd Dd dd	DD Dd Dd dd	DD Dd Dd dd
Female Fairway Parent	Dd	DD DD DD Dd	DD Dd Dd dd	DD Dd Dd dd	DD Dd Dd dd	DD Dd Dd dd	DD Dd Dd dd	DD Dd Dd dd	DD Dd Dd dd	DD Dd Dd dd	DD Dd Dd dd
	Dd	DD DD DD Dd	DD Dd Dd dd	DD Dd Dd dd	DD Dd Dd dd	DD Dd Dd dd	DD Dd Dd dd	DD Dd Dd dd	DD Dd Dd dd	DD Dd Dd dd	DD Dd Dd dd
	Dd	DD DD DD Dd	DD Dd Dd dd	DD Dd Dd dd	DD Dd Dd dd	DD Dd Dd dd	DD Dd Dd dd	DD Dd Dd dd	DD Dd Dd dd	DD Dd Dd dd	DD Dd Dd dd
	Dd	DD DD DD Dd	DD Dd Dd dd	DD Dd Dd dd	DD Dd Dd dd	DD Dd Dd dd	DD Dd Dd dd	DD Dd Dd dd	DD Dd Dd dd	DD Dd Dd dd	DD Dd Dd dd
	Dd	DD DD DD Dd	DD Dd Dd dd	DD Dd Dd dd	DD Dd Dd dd	DD Dd Dd dd	DD Dd Dd dd	DD Dd Dd dd	DD Dd Dd dd	DD Dd Dd dd	DD Dd Dd dd
	Dd	DD DD DD Dd	DD Dd Dd dd	DD Dd Dd dd	DD Dd Dd dd	DD Dd Dd dd	DD Dd Dd dd	DD Dd Dd dd	DD Dd Dd dd	DD Dd Dd dd	DD Dd Dd dd

Source: Sweeney and Danneberger (1997).

[a]The *DD, Dd,* and *dd* alleles add to 139 for 35%, 180 for 45%, and 81 for 20%, respectively.

Despite the fact that the annual bluegrass populations within this example are tetraploids, this matrix was established as if they were diploids; we believe that this is acceptable since only one of the two pairs of homologous chromosomes is thought to carry dominant and recessive genes for dormancy.

ways—in the frequency of RAPD markers, they concluded that all greens contained a single population, while the fairways contained several distinct populations, all different from the greens. They concluded that gene flow between greens and fairways was largely restricted. But physically moving genes, either through pollen or seeds, does not ensure that they will result in population changes, as new plants must become established and competitive members of the community for such changes to occur.

TABLE 2.3

Distribution of Gametes for Dormancy (*D*) and Nondormancy (*d*) among Annual Bluegrass Populations in a Green Producing Entirely Nondormant (*dd*) Seed and a Fairway Producing Entirely Dormant Seed in Which 90 Percent of the Plants Contain the Recessive (*d*) Allele[a]

		Male Fairway Parent									
		DD	Dd	Dd	Dd	Dd	Dd	Dd	Dd	Dd	Dd
Female Green Parent	dd	Dd Dd / Dd Dd	Dd Dd / dd dd	Dd Dd / dd dd	Dd Dd / dd dd	Dd Dd / dd dd	Dd Dd / dd dd	Dd Dd / dd dd	Dd Dd / dd dd	Dd Dd / dd dd	Dd Dd / dd dd
	dd	Dd Dd / Dd Dd	Dd Dd / dd dd	Dd Dd / dd dd	Dd Dd / dd dd	Dd Dd / dd dd	Dd Dd / dd dd	Dd Dd / dd dd	Dd Dd / dd dd	Dd Dd / dd dd	Dd Dd / dd dd
	dd	Dd Dd / Dd Dd	Dd Dd / dd dd	Dd Dd / dd dd	Dd Dd / dd dd	Dd Dd / dd dd	Dd Dd / dd dd	Dd Dd / dd dd	Dd Dd / dd dd	Dd Dd / dd dd	Dd Dd / dd dd
	dd	Dd Dd / Dd Dd	Dd Dd / dd dd	Dd Dd / dd dd	Dd Dd / dd dd	Dd Dd / dd dd	Dd Dd / dd dd	Dd Dd / dd dd	Dd Dd / dd dd	Dd Dd / dd dd	Dd Dd / dd dd
	dd	Dd Dd / Dd Dd	Dd Dd / dd dd	Dd Dd / dd dd	Dd Dd / dd dd	Dd Dd / dd dd	Dd Dd / dd dd	Dd Dd / dd dd	Dd Dd / dd dd	Dd Dd / dd dd	Dd Dd / dd dd
	dd	Dd Dd / Dd Dd	Dd Dd / dd dd	Dd Dd / dd dd	Dd Dd / dd dd	Dd Dd / dd dd	Dd Dd / dd dd	Dd Dd / dd dd	Dd Dd / dd dd	Dd Dd / dd dd	Dd Dd / dd dd
	dd	Dd Dd / Dd Dd	Dd Dd / dd dd	Dd Dd / dd dd	Dd Dd / dd dd	Dd Dd / dd dd	Dd Dd / dd dd	Dd Dd / dd dd	Dd Dd / dd dd	Dd Dd / dd dd	Dd Dd / dd dd
	dd	Dd Dd / Dd Dd	Dd Dd / dd dd	Dd Dd / dd dd	Dd Dd / dd dd	Dd Dd / dd dd	Dd Dd / dd dd	Dd Dd / dd dd	Dd Dd / dd dd	Dd Dd / dd dd	Dd Dd / dd dd
	dd	Dd Dd / Dd Dd	Dd Dd / dd dd	Dd Dd / dd dd	Dd Dd / dd dd	Dd Dd / dd dd	Dd Dd / dd dd	Dd Dd / dd dd	Dd Dd / dd dd	Dd Dd / dd dd	Dd Dd / dd dd
	dd	Dd Dd / Dd Dd	Dd Dd / dd dd	Dd Dd / dd dd	Dd Dd / dd dd	Dd Dd / dd dd	Dd Dd / dd dd	Dd Dd / dd dd	Dd Dd / dd dd	Dd Dd / dd dd	Dd Dd / dd dd

Source: Sweeney and Danneberger (1997).

[a]The *DD*, *Dd*, and *dd* alleles add to 0 for 0%, 220 for 55%, and 180 for 45%, respectively.

Despite the fact that the annual bluegrass populations within this example are tetraploids, this matrix was established as if they were diploids; we believe that this is acceptable since only one of the two pairs of homologous chromosomes is thought to carry dominant and recessive genes for dormancy.

SEASONAL GROWTH AND DEVELOPMENT

Cool-season turfgrasses typically show a bimodal growth pattern (Turgeon, 2002b). Shoot growth begins with a strong spring flush that eventually subsides and may slow even further with increasing summer temperatures. With the resumption of cooler temperatures in late summer and early fall, vertical shoot growth increases and is often accompanied by vigorous tillering. Because maximum root growth occurs at slightly lower temperatures than shoot growth, it is often observed earlier in spring and later in the fall. Summer rooting is relatively slow and shallow in most cool-season turfgrasses. The decline in summer growth—especially root growth—reflects increasing photorespiration rates during the summer months. Photorespiration occurs when oxygen (O_2) is consumed in place of carbon dioxide (CO_2) in the C_3 (Calvin) photosynthetic cycle, resulting in reduced PGA (phosphogyceric acid) production and the evolution of CO_2; thus, instead of CO_2 being fixed by the plant, it is released, reducing net photosynthesis. Photorespiration increases with increasing temperature, light intensity, and O_2 concentration. In full-sun locations with normal atmospheric O_2 concentrations (21 percent), temperature is the driving force in photorespiration. With increasing summer temperatures, photorespiration increases, resulting in reductions in photosynthetic efficiency, plant growth, and carbohydrate reserve levels. Since shoots can utilize locally produced carbohydrates, while roots must import them to sustain growth, the initial effect of limited or inadequate carbohydrate production is likely to be reduced root growth. Where shoot growth is aggressively promoted through irrigation and fertilization practices, an initially extensive root system may decline dramatically.

Seasonal growth of annual bluegrass varies somewhat from that typical of other cool-season turfgrasses in several important respects (Figure 2.7). The production of seed heads in spring affects aesthetic appearance and results in the utilization of carbohydrates to support flowering culm and inflorescence development, often at the expense of other plant portions. A vegetative shoot that has converted to a flowering shoot is destined to die, as the growing point has been elevated and transformed to form the inflorescence and can no longer produce leaf primordia. Thus, flowering shoots must be replaced with new shoots arising from axillary buds or germinating seeds. There is considerable anecdotal evidence that this phenomenon is also associated with a dramatic decline in root growth, resulting in the trimodal growth pattern shown in Figure 2.7. In contrast, Kentucky bluegrass shows the more typical bimodal growth pattern for both shoot and root growth (Figure 2.8) described earlier, and creeping bentgrass shows bimodal root growth with shoot growth more typical of that observed with warm-season turfgrass species (Figure 2.9) (Kosky, 1983).

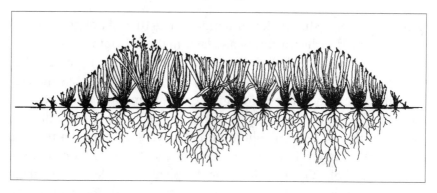

FIGURE 2.7 ■ *Seasonal growth of annual bluegrass showing bimodal shoot-growth and trimodal root-growth patterns.*

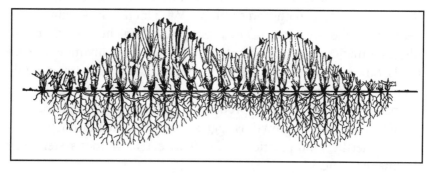

FIGURE 2.8 ■ *Seasonal growth of Kentucky bluegrass showing bimodal shoot- and root-growth patterns.*

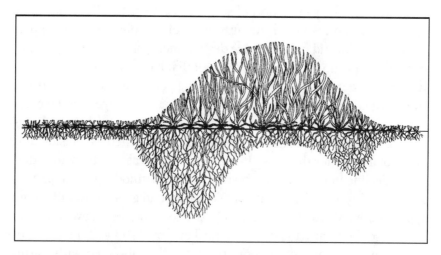

FIGURE 2.9 ■ *Seasonal growth of creeping bentgrass showing shoot-growth and bimodal root-growth patterns.*

COMPETITION

Competition may be defined as the interaction between individuals brought about by a shared requirement for a resource in limited supply, and leading to a reduction in the survivorship, growth, and/or reproduction of the individuals concerned (Begon et al., 1986). Although competition can occur at all levels within an ecosystem, we focus on two levels: population-based competition and community-based competition.

Population-Based (Intraspecific) Competition

The number of plants in a population that can be sustained on a particular site is governed by the carrying capacity of the environment in which it resides (Danneberger, 1993). The carrying capacity is determined by the availability of light, moisture, nutrients, and other resources essential for plant growth. Where these resources are sufficiently abundant that they do not limit plant growth, the plant population can achieve its maximum density. Population growth can be characterized by the *logistic equation* as

$$\frac{dN}{dt} = \frac{rN(K-N)}{K}$$

where N is the size of the population, dN/dt is the population growth rate (literally, the change in the population divided by the change in time), r is the potential rate at which a particular population can increase, and K is the carrying capacity (the maximum number of individuals that a particular habitat can support) of the system. Initial growth of a population depends on the size of the existing population (initial N) and the rate at which it can grow (r); however, the growth rate will decrease as the population approaches the carrying capacity (K). When N eventually reaches K, the population will have achieved its maximum density and will stop growing (i.e., $dN/dt = 0$).

Shoot density is typically higher in mowed turfgrass populations than in unmowed populations. Furthermore, within the mowing tolerance range of a particular turfgrass, shoot density is inversely related to mowing height. As a consequence, the highest attainable shoot densities are reached at the lowest sustainable mowing heights.

Physiology

Crowded populations of plants are governed by a principle of population biology called the *thinning rule*, which is based on the fact that at high densities the mean size of surviving plant shoots is reduced (competition-density effect); furthermore, the probability that these shoots will, in fact, survive is also reduced, leading to a self-thinning phenomenon by which population density is controlled and the size structure of the population is altered (Danneberger, 1993; Firbank and Watkinson, 1990; Lush, 1988b and 1990). This aspect of competition is called *intraspecific competition*, as only one plant species—and often only a single subspecies of plants—may be involved. In an annual blue-grass population, shoot density increases in direct proportion to increases in the carrying capacity of the environment; once maximum density is reached, the addition of each new shoot is matched by the loss of an existing shoot, so that shoot density is sustained at a constant level. Under the thinning rule, the competitive stress accompanying increasing shoot density leads to decreasing shoot size, and thus higher shoot density, until the maximum number of the smallest surviving shoots is reached. Also, as a population develops following germination, the frequency of individual plant weights shifts from a normal distribution to one that is skewed, with mostly small individuals and perhaps a few large ones. The relatively few large plants occur most likely where voids develop from mechanical injury or pests, followed by recovery from the growth of adjacent plants which are initially larger and coarser textured than plants under competitive stress.

The mechanism by which plant populations adhere to the thinning rule is based on the ability of neighboring shoots to sense each other's presence by sensing far-red radiation reflected from or transmitted through nearby leaves. Solar radiation is rich in red light compared with far-red light; however, light that is reflected or transmitted by neighboring leaves is altered and contains a relatively high proportion of far-red light. Red light converts phytochrome, a pigment contained in plant cells, from an inactive (P_r) to an active (P_{fr}) form, and far-red light returns phytochrome back to its inactive form. Active phytochrome regulates plant growth and development, presumably by regulating the biosynthesis of selected phyto-hormones (in this case, gibberellic acid). When converted to the inactive form, however, growth and developmental processes are altered, resulting in thinner leaves, reduced density and tillering, shallower rooting, thinner cuticles, and lower reserve carbohydrates. Consequently, dense plant populations in which neighboring leaves shade each other apparently adjust their growth, and thus adhere to the thinning rule, through the activity of light-mediated phytohormones.

Community-Based (Interspecific) Competition

Competition within mixed communities is more complex than that in monocultures, as the different species may have different resource requirements, different patterns of growth, respond differently to environmental conditions, and modify the environment for each other (Firbank and Watkinson, 1990). The degree of inequality among individuals in mixtures is related to the ability of one species to outcompete the other. Where two species are evenly matched, size inequality is similar to that observed in monocultures.

Two mechanisms of community-based competition have been described: direct interference and resource competition (Connell, 1990; Tilman, 1990). Direct interference involves one individual directly harming a neighbor in various ways, including release of toxic substances, called *allelopathic interaction,* and direct overgrowth, with the consequent capacity to obtain more of the available light. Allelopathic competition would be influenced by the rate at which the competitive species made the allelopathic compound; the effects of the compound on growth, survival, and/or reproduction; and the rate of loss or decay of the compound. Currently, there is no evidence that allelopathic competition is involved in mixed turfgrass communities containing annual bluegrass; however, this aspect of competition cannot be entirely discounted. Direct overgrowth, however, is a common phenomenon in turfgrass communities containing annual bluegrass. In a field study at the University of Illinois, annual bluegrass populations were overgrown by Kentucky bluegrass and tall fescue at 3-in. (7.6-cm) and 1.5-in. (3.8-cm) mowing heights, but persisted and predominated where a ¾-in. (1.9-cm) mowing height was employed (Turgeon and Vargas, 1979). Also, greens-type annual bluegrass selections planted into creeping bentgrass turfs maintained under a fairway-type intensity of culture in a study at University Park, Pennsylvania, were quickly overgrown by the bentgrasses, indicating that direct overgrowth can indeed occur in some annual bluegrass–creeping bentgrass communities (Turgeon, 2002a).

Resource competition can be further divided into competition for soil resources and competition for light. Soil resource competition is dependent on growth and reproduction of each competing species, the dynamics of resource supply, and nutrient consumption rates. The success of one competitor over another may reflect a greater ability to acquire resources where the supply is limited, or to utilize these resources efficiently where the supply is abundant (Grime, 1977; Tilman, 1990). For example, deeper-rooted species have a competitive advantage over shallower-rooted plants in obtaining moisture and nutrients from deeper soil regions where evapotranspiration, volatilization, or leaching have depleted the surface layer of soil of its supply of these resources. This competitive advantage is lost, however, where these resources are provided at frequencies sufficient to ensure their continuous availability.

With respect to moisture, annual bluegrass and creeping bentgrass have a higher moisture requirement than Kentucky bluegrass (Danneberger, 1993); however, under conditions where the soil water table was high, the root systems of annual bluegrass and Kentucky bluegrass were shallower than that of creeping bentgrass (Waddington and Zimmerman, 1972) and the submersion tolerance of creeping bentgrass was superior to that of Kentucky bluegrass and annual bluegrass (Beard and Martin, 1970). In poorly drained compacted soils, however, annual bluegrass exhibited better tolerance of oxygen-deficient conditions than other turfgrasses (Carrow and Petrovic, 1992; Van Wijk et al., 1977; Waddington et al., 1978; Youngner, 1959).

With respect to nutrients, annual bluegrass was found to be more competitive in communities with several cool-season turfgrasses as the rates of nitrogen, phosphorus, and potassium fertilization increased (Adams, 1980; Danneberger, 1993; Dest and Allinson, 1981; Escritt and Legg, 1970; Goss et al., 1975; Sprague and Burton, 1937; Waddington et al., 1978); however, Wehner and Watschke (1981) found that the heat tolerance of annual bluegrass decreased with increasing nitrogen fertilization, while Dest and Allinson (1981) reported that phorphorus applications should be adjusted upward with increasing rates of applied nitrogen to maximize survival. Since injury to annual bluegrass can occur at soil salinity levels as low as 3 dS/m or lower, care should be taken to ensure that fertilization practices do not result in toxic concentrations of soluble salts (Harivandi et al., 1992).

Soil pH affects the availability of nutrients and may influence the competitive ability of annual bluegrass in mixed turfgrass communities (Danneberger, 1993). Bentgrasses are generally considered more tolerant of moderately acid soils, whereas bluegrasses appear to grow better at pH values near neutral. Applications of sulfur have been used with some success to reduce soil pH and discourage annual bluegrass in mixed communities with creeping bentgrass (Goss et al., 1975); however, excessive use of acid-forming materials can also adversely affect the growth and quality of bentgrasses and other turfgrass species (Sprague and Burton, 1937). Juska and Hanson (1969) found that the growth of annual bluegrass improved when the pH of a loamy sand was increased from 4.5 to 6.5, but no effect was noted on a silt loam; the same pH change improved the growth of Kentucky bluegrass on both soils. Annual bluegrass encroachment into bermudagrass turf during the cool season increased from 0 to 63 percent as soil pH increased from 5.0 to 5.8 (Sartain, 1985).

With respect to light, shade favors annual bluegrass over creeping bentgrass and other species that are not very shade tolerant. Thus, tree-shaded greens tend to have more annual bluegrass than greens in full-sun locations. Even within a turfgrass canopy, shading from the upper leaves may influence the growth and competitive ability of plants within the turfgrass community (refer to the earlier discussion of intraspecific competition).

Photoperiod may also influence the relative growth and thus the competitive ability of competing plant species. Brede (1982) showed that the tillering rate of annual bluegrass and Kentucky bluegrass were the same under a 10-hour photoperiod. Annual bluegrass tillered four times faster under a 15-hour photoperiod.

In addition to the factors described so far, community-based competition can be greatly affected by temperature. While the tolerance of annual bluegrass to temperature extremes is below that of Kentucky bluegrass and creeping bentgrass (Beard, 1973), optimum growth of annual bluegrass occurs at temperatures that are generally lower than those considered optimum for Kentucky bluegrass and creeping bentgrass. Comparisons of seasonal growth curves for annual bluegrass (Figures 2.7) with Kentucky bluegrass (Figure 2.8)

and creeping bentgrass (Figure 2.9) show that annual bluegrass typically initiates shoot and root growth earlier in the spring and sustains
its growth later in the fall. In research conducted on a green composed of creeping bentgrass and annual bluegrass in southeastern
Australia, Lush (1988a) found that the creeping bentgrass/annual
bluegrass shoot ratio was 2:1 in summer and 1:2 in winter, suggesting that the growth of annual bluegrass was favored in the winter half
of the year, whereas the growth of creeping bentgrass was favored in
the summer half. In spaced plants, the tillering capacity of annual
bluegrass exceeded that of creeping bentgrass from late fall, enabling
annual bluegrass to become dominant by midwinter. Conversely,
creeping bentgrass grew more aggressively than annual bluegrass
after early spring and became dominant by late spring. These results
suggest that the differential in the seasonal competitive ability of
creeping bentgrass and annual bluegrass reflected the relative birth
rates of tillers.

Finally, whenever there are voids within a turfgrass community,
a potentially competitive plant species may occupy the voids and subsequently compete with adjacent plant populations (Watschke and
Schmidt, 1992). For example, voids created within a creeping
bentgrass green from ball marks, disease, or dying weeds may be
filled by bentgrass plants from lateral shoot growth of adjacent
plants; however, they also permit the introduction of other plant species, such as annual bluegrass, from germination of resident or transported seeds or from vegetative growth of adjacent plants already
present within the plant community. Early successional annuals,
such as the annual biotypes of annual bluegrass, are competitively
superior in habitats in which high disturbance rates cause a high ratio
of light to soil resources (Grace, 1990). In contrast, later successional
species are competitively superior where low disturbance rates allow
light to become scarce and the ratio of light to soil resources to
decline. This is consistent with turfgrass sites that have been disturbed and provide invasion ports for weeds, including annual biotypes of annual bluegrass, versus the predominance of perennial
biotypes in closed communities where full canopies limit light penetration to the soil surface.

CHAPTER 3
Annual Bluegrass
Culture

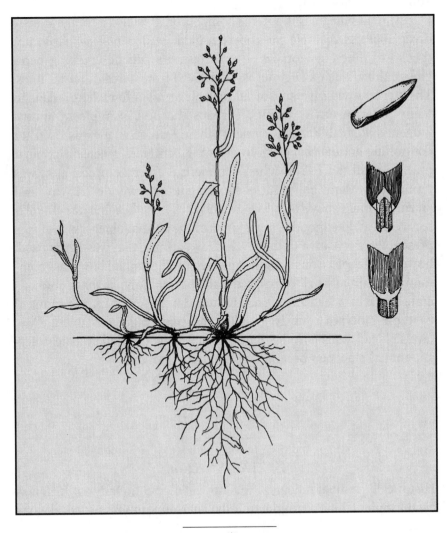

NUMEROUS STUDIES have been done on the cultural requirements of creeping bentgrass as well as other "desirable grasses."
Most of the research on annual bluegrass has been on how to
eliminate it from mixed stands. Discussed below is the best information available on the cultural requirements for sustaining healthy
annual bluegrass turf.

Annual bluegrass is a fierce competitor. It is also a tremendously
diverse species. A single golf course could have dozens—perhaps hun-
dreds—of different biotypes. In contrast, a synthetic creeping bentgrass cultivar such as Penncross is derived from three different lines.
The tremendous diversity of annual bluegrass allows it to adapt to
many different environments. Perhaps the best example of annual
bluegrass adaptability was evident where lead arsenate was used for
controlling annual bluegrass in creeping bentgrass greens, a popular
practice until the 1970s, when commercial arsenate production was
terminated. Many golf course superintendents wondered why lead
arsenic worked so well for five to ten years, then became largely ineffective. In all likelihood, the majority of the annual bluegrass biotypes
present were sensitive to the level of lead arsenic that was being used;
however, the selection pressure imposed on the annual bluegrass community eventually led to the predominance of biotypes that could tolerate the level of lead arsenic accumulated in the green. Seed produced
by these biotypes resulted in offspring that could also tolerate the
levels of lead arsenic in the greens. Eventually, the lead arsenic–tolerant annual bluegrass became the dominant biotype.

ESTABLISHMENT

Cultivar Selection

Historically, annual bluegrass was not used intentionally for turfgrass
establishment but occurred naturally where environmental conditions

favored its development and persistence in turfs originally established with other turfgrass species. With rapid and sustained evolutionary development from intraspecific hybridization and selection pressure, natural varieties of annual bluegrass developed over time that formed higher-quality and more persistent turfs than those resulting from the initial invaders. Some annual bluegrass selections acquired from old greens have been studied and several have been released for commercial distribution. The first, called Petersen's creeping bluegrass, was released by the Minnesota Agricultural Experiment Station. Creeping bluegrass and *Poa reptans* were proposed as the common and Latin names, respectively, to differentiate this grass from wild-type annual bluegrasses; however, although the proposed common name may persist, there is some question about the appropriateness of the proposed Latin name, as *Poa annua* f. *reptans* is the generally recognized scientific designation for this grass.

Active breeding programs in Minnesota and Pennsylvania will probably produce many other commercial cultivars, especially given the superior performance of some selections in field trials. In a study conducted at Pennsylvania State University, several greens-type annual bluegrass selections showed outstanding persistence and competitive capacity in mixed communities with creeping bentgrasses, with one of the selections increasing in diameter nearly two-fold over the four-year experimental period (Turgeon, 2002a).

Propagation

Annual bluegrass occurs naturally as creeping bentgrass or other turfgrasses are invaded under conditions favorable for annual bluegrass growth and development. Sometimes small plugs of annual bluegrass extracted from coring operations are used intentionally for establishment. These new turfs are usually "nurseries" that are subsequently used as sources of sod for establishing new greens, tees, or fairways.

PRIMARY CULTURAL OPERATIONS

Mowing

Greens

Annual bluegrass can tolerate very low heights of cut. It survives at mowing heights below ⅛ in. (3.2 mm), making it an ideal turfgrass for putting greens, especially where putting speed is important. It maintains its density at this low mowing height because of the enormous competition-density effect evident in many greens-type annual bluegrass biotypes. This also enhances its resistance to invasion by weeds or other grasses. Annual bluegrass may also produce viable seed when mowed below $\frac{1}{8}$ in. (3.2 mm). To avoid scalping injury and to minimize environmental stress, annual bluegrass greens should be mowed at least six times per week.

Fairways

Although some annual bluegrasses survive well at fairway mowing heights between $\frac{3}{8}$ in. (9.5 mm) and $\frac{7}{8}$ in. (22.2 mm), its fairway quality is optimized at mowing heights below $\frac{1}{2}$ in. (12.7 mm). Fairways should be mowed at least three times per week, with five to six times preferred.

The use of lightweight fairway mowers and the removal of clippings has led in some instances to an increase in the creeping bentgrass population, with corresponding decreases in annual bluegrass. With highly compacted soils, however, fairways may remain predominantly annual bluegrass. Under these circumstances the use of lightweight mowers and, more important, the collecting of clippings during warm weather have greatly increased the quality and density of annual bluegrass fairways.

Roughs

Although annual bluegrass may persist at mowing heights of between 1½ in. (38.1 mm) and 3 in. (76.2 mm), it is often clumpy and unsightly and may not survive except where poor drainage or insufficient sunlight limits the survival or competitive growth of other turfgrass species.

Fertilization

While high nitrogen rates could promote excessive growth and render annual bluegrass more susceptible to summer stresses, it responds well to moderate levels of nitrogen fertility (Danneberger et al., 1983). In addition to its role in sustaining healthy growth, nitrogen is important for managing the two most important diseases of annual bluegrass, anthracnose and summer patch, by increasing the plants' natural resistance to the diseases and by enhancing the efficacy of the fungicides used for their control (Danneberger et al., 1983; Vargas, 1994).

Nitrogen for Greens

Ideally, annual bluegrass greens would receive from 2 to 3 lb of nitrogen (N) per 1000 ft^2 (0.98 to 1.46 kg N per 100 m^2) during the warm summer months (June through September in the northern hemisphere). In the cooler growing months of spring and fall, they would receive up to an additional 1 to 1.5 lb N per 1000 ft^2 (0.49 to 0.73 kg N per 100 m^2) each season. This amounts to between 4 and 6 lb N per 1000 ft^2 (1.92 to 2.93 kg N per 100 m^2) for the entire growing season. To sustain plant health and maintain high putting speeds, these quantities of nitrogen must be supplied in small amounts over multiple applications; thus, "spoon-feeding" greens with light applications—usually made with a sprayer—of primarily water-soluble fertilizers would require weekly rates of $\frac{1}{6}$ to $\frac{1}{4}$ lb N per 1000 ft^2 (0.08 to 0.12 kg N per 100 m^2) or biweekly rates of $\frac{1}{3}$ to $\frac{1}{2}$ lb N per 1000 ft^2 (0.16 to 0.24 kg N per 100 m^2).

A portion of the total nitrogen requirement could be met with an application of 1 lb N per 1000 ft^2 (0.49 kg N per 100 m^2) in midfall, just after the annual bluegrass population has ceased vertical shoot growth (usually around November 1 in Michigan). This "dormant" fertilization can be made with a portion—perhaps up to 50 percent—of the N from slowly available carriers.

Nitrogen for Fairways and Tees

Annual bluegrass fairways and tees require approximately the same amount of nitrogen fertility as do greens. The amount may vary depending on whether clippings are removed or returned and, if removed, the number of months during the growing season this is done. A good rule of thumb for fairways is: Where clippings are returned, about 25 percent less nitrogen is required than where clippings are removed. Granular fertilizers are generally better suited for use on fairways and tees, as putting speed is not a concern.

Phosphorus and Potassium

The amount of phosphorus and potassium needed for healthy annual bluegrass can be determined by soil testing. Many golf course superintendents believe, however, that by routinely adding potassium in a 1:1 ratio with nitrogen, they have healthier or more stress-tolerant annual bluegrass during summer and winter. Also, to the extent that some annual bluegrass may be lost from traffic-induced injury, diseases, insects, and natural environmental stresses, having sufficient concentrations of available phosphorus in the soil helps to ensure successful reestablishment of annual bluegrass from its reservoir of seed accumulated in the soil.

Irrigation

Historically, agronomists have recommended intensive irrigations that moisten the turfgrass root zone thoroughly, while cautioning against applying water at rates in excess of the infiltration capacity of the turf to avoid standing water in depressions (i.e., puddling) and runoff of excess water downslope. Also recommended were long intervals between successive irrigations to allow the soil to dry out and thus maximize exchanges between atmospheric air and soil air, as this was thought to result in a more favorable soil environment for plant root growth. Moisture retained at deeper soil depths was thought to replenish root zone moisture, as water moves upward along the water-potential gradient created by surface soil drying. But soil water movement along a water-potential gradient is limited to the hydraulic conductivity of the soil, which often is far slower than the rate at which water is being removed from the root zone by actively transpiring plants. Also, because of high rates of photorespiration that reduce net photoassimilate production by cool-season turfgrasses under high summer temperatures, carbohydrate reserves may become very limited during the summer months (Turgeon, 2002b). As a consequence, root growth is often highly restricted, while root senescence may be accelerated during the summer, especially in intensively cultured cool-season turfgrasses such as annual bluegrass. Given the reality of such shallow root systems and the slowness with which water moves along a water potential gradient within the soil, the validity of the *intensive and infrequent approach* to turfgrass irrigation for intensively cultured turfs should be reexamined.

An alternative *light and frequent approach* has emerged that merits serious consideration. This approach is directed at meeting the moisture requirements of a shallow-rooted turfgrass community by providing just the right amount of moisture on a daily basis, thus minimizing the heat and drought stresses to which the turf would otherwise be subjected. By providing a more-or-less continuous supply of water, very high shoot densities can be sustained. With rapid drying, equally rapid exchanges between atmospheric air and soil air help to sustain a favorable soil environment for root respiration and soil-organism growth.

The ideal time to irrigate an intensively cultured annual bluegrass turf may be during the middle of the day, when heat and drought stresses are sometimes severe and of increasing concern as the day progresses. Regardless of the timing of irrigation, ensuring that the precipitation rate does not exceed the infiltration capacity of the turf is especially important for avoiding excessive soil moisture levels and associated problems, such as increased traffic-induced soil compaction and wear, poor root growth, and increased disease potential.

In addition to transpirational cooling from the water absorbed by plant roots, direct evaporative cooling from light midday irrigation can help shallow-rooted turfgrasses survive heat and drought stresses while keeping the turf drier for better playability. Some highly successful golf turf managers in humid climates with relatively frequent summer rainfall events rarely employ intensive irrigation; they rely primarily on frequent light irrigations and daytime syringing to sustain their annual bluegrass greens during the summer.

SUPPLEMENTARY CULTURAL OPERATIONS

Cultivation

Core Cultivation

Annual bluegrass turf should be core cultivated several times each year. While hollow-tine cultivation (HTC) to a depth of approximately 3 in. (7.6 cm) is the form most commonly employed, solid-tine cultivation (STC) is gaining in popularity. STC employs long, thin, solid tines that after penetrating the soil to their maximum depth, may uplift and fracture the soil mass during extraction, sometimes resulting in substantial increases in soil macroporosity. The beneficial effects of STC are most pronounced when the operation is done in dry soils; conversely, if soil moisture is high during STC, no improvements in soil macroporosity may occur. High-powered equipment now exists for performing HTC and STC to depths of up to 12 in. (30.5 cm) or more in the soil. The Verti-Drain is a commercially available deep-tine cultivation unit that may be employed to achieve these depths.

Favorable times for core cultivation during the growing season include (1) shortly after greenup in the spring, (2) immediately following the massive seed head production period in midspring, (3) after the summer stress period has ended and cool nighttime temperatures (<59°F, <15°C) have returned, and (4) late in the growing season when shoot growth has slowed substantially and root growth is active.

If core cultivation could be done only once, it probably should be done after the massive seed head production period in midspring. At this time, the annual bluegrass population has had several weeks without any new root initiation, as most of the photoassimilates have been directed to supporting seed head production. As a consequence, there may be only 2 to 3 weeks in which to develop new roots and store photoassimilate reserves before soil temperatures rise to the level at which new root initiation either slows dramatically or stops completely. Core cultivation immediately following the massive seed head production period will stimulate the plants to produce new shoots and roots while substantially improving soil aeration to support vigorous root growth in the immediate vicinity of the holes.

Where core cultivation is done early in the growing season, root and shoot growth are encouraged in the immediate vicinity of the channels created in the top few inches of soil and plants are better able to survive the coming summer stress period.

Late summer core cultivation of greens can help to relieve summer compaction and supply a better rooting medium for annual bluegrass. Opening up the turf canopy will encourage annual bluegrass seed to germinate and contribute new members to the turfgrass community. This is also the time when the cultivation process, coupled with heavy applications of topdressing soil, can seriously disrupt both routine and tournament play. Cultivation and topdressing can be especially annoying to golfers if the greens are already in excellent condition. For this reason many superintendents avoid core cultivation at this time, preferring to wait until later in the fall when play drops off due to cold weather.

Midfall is an excellent time to core annual bluegrass greens and fairways. While a considerable amount of lifting of the turf's surface can occur and interfere with putting on greens and lies on fairways, delaying core cultivation until after the prime golfing season is over takes advantage of the overwintering period for settling to occur and the surfaces to return to proper playing condition. An objection to late-season core cultivation is that the holes may not heal quickly due to slow shoot growth, and that exposed plant tissues may desiccate from drying winds, especially if topdressing soil is not applied to fill the holes completely. The increasing popularity of late-season core cultivation, however, is a testimony to the effectiveness of this practice in encouraging healthy root growth. Late-season core cultivation can also lead to substantial improvements in soil structure and aeration porosity, due to enhanced effects from freezing-and-thawing and wetting-and-drying cycles during the overwintering period.

Vertical Mowing

Vertical mowing is normally employed to remove grain from a green. Since there is very little grain in an annual bluegrass green, vertical mowing is usually not necessary for this purpose. Annual bluegrass greens can achieve very high shoot densities and become puffy, however, when lateral shoot growth has been vigorous. Putting speed and quality can be adversely affected under these conditions. Light vertical mowing can increase putting speed and quality by reducing shoot density and puffiness.

Vertical mowing on annual bluegrass greens and fairways, especially in early spring, can be employed to remove some of the older plants and allow juvenile plants to develop. This rejuvenation of the turf can enhance summer-stress tolerance and survival.

Spiking and Slicing

Spiking is a process by which small perforations are made to improve water infiltration in compacted greens. *Slicing* is a similar process employed principally on fairways. Both processes can be employed to break up surface crusts where these occur; however, they should not be done very often, as excessive spiking or slicing can lead to substantial thinning of the turf during periods of severe heat and drought stresses.

Rolling

Rolling greens to improve turf quality or to increase green speed has become very popular. Frequent rolling of creeping bentgrass greens can be problematic because of the potential for severe compaction of soil-based greens. Although annual bluegrass is more tolerant of soil compaction, excessive rolling can cause severe wear and reduce the turf's tolerance of heat and drought stresses.

Plant Growth Regulators

Plant growth regulators (PGRs) are compounds that regulate or alter turfgrass growth and development. Early versions of PGRs were used primarily to reduce mowing frequency; however, because of significant injury often resulting from their application, their use was largely restricted to utility turfs along roadsides and airport runways. Newer classes of PGRs introduced during the 1980s and 1990s are generally safer and have a broader range of effectiveness, thus their use has been extended to sports and lawn turfs. In addition to reducing vertical shoot growth (and thus mowing frequency), some PGRs can be used to achieve and sustain higher shoot densities and green speeds, selectively inhibit annual bluegrass growth in mixed communities with other turfgrasses, and inhibit or reduce seed head development.

PGRs were divided originally into two types: Type I for compounds that inhibit cell division and differentiation in meristematic regions of the plant, and Type II for compounds that inhibit plant growth by inhibiting gibberellin biosynthesis, thus causing reductions in cell elongation (Kaufmann, 1986; Watschke, 1985). Later, Watschke and DiPaola (1995) expanded the number of compounds considered as PGRs and proposed five classes (A through E), based on their respective modes of action (Table 3.1).

TABLE 3.1

Plant Growth Regulators Used on Annual Bluegrass

Generic Name	Trade Name	Class[a]	Type[b]	Uptake
Trinexpac-ethyl	Primo Primo Maxx Triple Play	A	II	Shoot
Paclobutrazol	Trimmit Turf Enhancer TGR	B	II	Root
Flurprimidol	Cutless	B	I	Root
Mefluidide	Embark 2S Embark T&O	C		Shoot
Sulfometuron-methyl	Oust	D		Shoot
Glyphosate	Roundup Pro	D		Shoot
Ethofumesate	Progress	D		Shoot
Ethephon	Proxy	E		Shoot
Gibberellic acid	RhyzUP	E		Shoot

[a] Class A = cell elongation inhibitor late in gibberellin biosynthesis pathway
Class B = cell elongation inhibitor early in gibberellin biosynthesis pathway
Class C = cell-division (mitotic) inhibitor
Class D = herbicide with growth-regulating properties at low rates of application
Class E = phytohormone
[b] Older system of classification

Class A

These are compounds that inhibit gibberellic-acid biosynthesis *late* in the pathway. Trinexapac-ethyl is the only compound in this class. It is the most widely used of all the PGRs on golf turfs. Trinexapac-ethyl is foliar absorbed and has no soil residual activity. A 1-hour rain-free period is required after application to ensure adequate absorption. Mowing can be performed as early as one day following application without reducing its efficacy. Trinexapac-ethyl is primarily used on fairways to reduce clippings and improve uniformity. A darker green turfgrass color following the use of this compound is a secondary benefit. Trinexapac-ethyl is also used on greens to improve mowing quality, increase density, and provide more consistent putting speed over time. It has also been shown to increase the shade tolerance of some turfs. Trinexapac-ethyl is not effective for selectively suppressing annual bluegrass when grown in combination with creeping bentgrass, as this compound will improve the turf quality of both species. Trinexapac-ethyl does not suppress the production of annual bluegrass seed heads, but does reduce their height.

Class B

These are compounds that inhibit gibberellic-acid biosynthesis *early* in the pathway. Paclobutrazol and flurprimidol are both Class-B PGRs. Their uptake and activity are so similar that they can be described jointly. These compounds are root absorbed and primarily used in annual bluegrass–creeping bentgrass fairway conversion programs. They suppress the growth of annual bluegrass to a greater degree than that of creeping bentgrass, thus providing a competitive advantage that may enable creeping bentgrass eventually to dominate the turfgrass community. Class-B PGRs cause significant discoloration of annual bluegrass and a widening of the leaf blades of creeping bentgrass. Although repeat applications have been very effective in converting annual bluegrass–creeping bentgrass fairways (as well as collars) to predominately creeping bentgrass turfs, they have not been as effective on greens. Class-B PGRs are very similar in chemical structure to some of the DMI fungicides, which explains the limited dollar spot control that often results from their use. Using Class-B PGRs in combination with the DMI fungicides has been reported to cause unacceptable injury to the turf. As with Class-A PGRs, the

Class-B compounds do not suppress the production of annual blue-grass seed heads, but do reduce their height.

Class C

These are compounds that inhibit cell division in meristematic regions of the plant. Maleic hydrazide, amidochlor, and mefluidide are Class-C PGRs. Of these only mefluidide has widespread use on golf turfs. It is absorbed through both the foliage and the roots. The primary use of mefluidide is to reduce the massive seed head formation that occurs on annual bluegrass during spring (Figure 3.1, see color insert). Growing-degree-day models can be useful for predicting proper application timing. In the model developed by Danneberger and Vargas (1984), growing-degree-days are accumulated following the first mowing. Growing-degree-days are calculated by averaging daily maximum and minimum temperatures and subtracting the base (55°F) temperature. If the result of this calculation is a positive number it is added to the previous day's total. Any result that is negative is recorded as zero. The mefluidide application is made when 25 growing-degree-days have accumulated. Applications will continue to be effective up to 50 growing-degree-days. After this time, the effectiveness of mefluidide applications will diminish rapidly. Turfgrass discoloration associated with mefluidide applications can be mitigated somewhat by applying a cheated iron product prior to the mefluidide application. Tank mixing iron and mefluidide reduces the efficacy of mefluidide in suppressing annual bluegrass seed-head formation. The discoloration from mefluidide is temporary and will be followed by a period of dark-green growth of the turfgrass as the effects of the PGR wear off. In some instances the inhibition seed-head formation from the use of mefluidide has lead to a better developed root system (Street et al., 1984) (Figure 3.2, see color insert).

Class D

These are herbicides used at sublethal rates to selectively suppress the growth of some species in mixed turfgrass communities. For example, very low rates [0.18 to 0.22 lb active ingredient (a.i.) per acre or 0.20 to 0.25 kg a.i. per ha] of glyphosate have been used to injure annual bluegrass selectively in mixed stands with creeping bentgrass. Other herbicides in this group include sulfometuron-methyl and ethofumesate. The growth-regulating effects from these applications can be seen in the annual bluegrass survivors that tend to exhibit earlier spring green up, stunted growth, and fewer seed heads the following season. *Xanthomonas campestris,* a biological control for annual bluegrass, has elicited similar survivor responses.

Class E

These are synthetically produced phytohormones or chemical formulations that are hydrolyzed into phytohormones by treated plants. Ethephon and gibberellic acid are Class-E PGRs. Ethephon is a foliar-absorbed commercial formulation that generates ethylene in treated plants. Like mefluidide it is primarily used to prevent annual bluegrass seed-head formation. It can provide growth regulation and seed-head suppression for up to 7 weeks. The application timing of ethephon is not well understood; however, it appears that it must be applied earlier than mefluidide. Whereas mefluidide is almost exclusively used to prevent the massive seed-head production of annual bluegrass in the spring, ethephon can be applied throughout the season in cooler climates where annual bluegrass dominates and tends to produce sporadic seed heads all season long. Repeat applications on annual bluegrass have resulted in increased density, upright shoot orientation, and overall improved summer vigor. However, turf treated with ethephon typically demonstrates a light-green (Granny Smith apple) color, which some people find objectionable. This effect is not as noticeable on annual bluegrass as it is normally more yellow than other species; thus, ethephon is especially suited for use on turfs that are predominantly annual bluegrass. To overcome this discoloration, some superintendents have tank mixed ethephon and trinexapac-ethyl. Gibberellic-acid can be applied, where necessary, to counter the effects of such gibberellic-acid biosynthesis inhibitors and the Class-A and Class-B PGR.

Controlling Winter Injury

Although annual bluegrass is adapted to a broad array of climatic conditions, it generally does best in regions with relatively mild summer and winter temperatures. Severe winters and their accompanying stresses can be threatening to stands of annual bluegrass, especially where ice forms and persists for prolonged periods. Beard (1964, 1966, 1973) showed that after 75 days under ice, annual bluegrass typically dies, whereas creeping bentgrass can survive for at least 120 days under continuous ice cover. The loss of annual bluegrass may be due to low-oxygen (hypoxic) and oxygen-depleted (anoxic) conditions, as well as to the buildup of toxic gases (CO_2, ethanol), under the ice. In areas where alternate freezing and thawing of standing water lead to high plant hydration levels, ice crystals can form in the cells of annual bluegrass crowns, causing the death of entire plants. Also, ice encasement of plant cells can cause extensive turfgrass damage, even at low internal hydration levels (Hamilton, 2001). Ice-related damage to annual bluegrass is often more severe in shaded areas. Although this may be due to more prolonged coverage of snow and ice in the shade, it may also reflect the effects of reduced irradiance on plant hardiness and, perhaps, the lower nonstructural carbohydrate levels of shaded plants.

To ensure that death associated with ice damage in winter is avoided, ice formations should be broken up and removed. Breaking up ice formations on greens and leaving the pieces in place may be worse than simply leaving the ice undisturbed. To the extent that breaking up ice contributes to its melting and subsequent refreezing in place, crown hydration and subsequent death of annual bluegrass plants are actually favored. If refreezing does not occur and the standing water eventually drains away, ice-related injury will not occur. In Michigan during the winter of 1981, a severe ice storm knocked out power for over a week in some places. Between 4 and 6 in. (10 to 15 cm) of ice were deposited over entire golf courses. Superintendents who went out in January when the temperatures were still below freezing and broke up the ice and removed it from their greens had very little ice-related injury. Those who did nothing at all also had very little injury when the ice finally melted in mid-March. However, superintendents who broke up the ice where it melted and refroze in early March suffered severe turf loss. Similar incidences have been observed throughout the years in northern-tier U.S. states and Canada. It appears the best solution to avoid ice-related damage on annual bluegrass turfs is to break up and remove the ice when daytime temperatures are below freezing. The next best choice is to do nothing and hope that ice melt is followed by nighttime temperatures that don't go below freezing for a couple of days. During ice melt, it is advisable to squeegee standing water from the green. Of course, improving surface drainage can substantially reduce the potential for ice-related damage to annual bluegrass greens, as internal drainage is nonexistent in frozen greens.

Canadian researchers found that annual bluegrass greens subjected to alternating freezing and thawing conditions rapidly lost proteins associated with cold tolerance and died when freezing temperatures returned (Dionne et al., 1999). Conversely, greens that were mulched to minimize temperature fluctuations had less cold-tolerance protein loss and survived.

In late 1997 and early 1998, the upper midwestern United States experienced one of the mildest winters on record. Freezing temperatures in late January and early February were followed by warm weather, with temperatures reaching above 70°F (21°C). This should have caused the plants to lose their cold-tolerance proteins; however, below-freezing temperatures in late February resulted in very little turf loss. If loss of cold-tolerance proteins were the only factor involved in the loss of annual bluegrass to cold injury, the turf should have died. Presumably, survival of the annual bluegrass was due to the lack of ice on the greens. Ice and crown hydration appear to be major contributors to loss of annual bluegrass during winter.

Perhaps the best way to avoid ice damage to greens is to prevent ice from forming on the turf through the use of protective covers installed in the fall after the last mowing and removed the following spring (Dionne et al., 1999). Excelsior mats, for example, can be used for up to three years before replacement is required. Although they are expensive and require a large storage area, they are less expensive than replacing dead grass. Solid covers can also be used. This method usually involves placing a perforated cover on the greens, then straw, and finally a solid cover on top of the straw. The problem with this method is stabilizing the covers to prevent their loss during heavy winds.

Finally, it is important to maintain adequate phosphorus and potassium levels through fertilization, as both of these elements are used to increase cellular osmotic potential during hardening.

PEST MANAGEMENT

Weeds

Despite the seeming paradox of controlling weeds in turfgrass communities dominated by annual bluegrass, itself a "weed" of long-term notoriety, an annual bluegrass turf can be invaded by an assortment of weeds that detract from its visual and functional quality. Summer annual grasses, mainly crabgrass and goosegrass, can invade when annual bluegrass is under the stress of seed production in late spring and environmental stress in the summer. Similarly, most other perennial grasses, such as creeping bentgrass, have a competitive advantage over annual bluegrass during the summer months. Broadleaf species, primarily white clover and mouse-ear chickweed, exploit any opportunity to invade an annual bluegrass turf whenever conditions favor their germination and growth.

Effective weed control requires an annual bluegrass community that is healthy and growing vigorously, and thus naturally resistant to invasion by other plant species. Therefore, creating and maintaining conditions that favor healthy growth, including ensuring proper drainage and providing adequate moisture and fertility, are necessary for preventing weed invasion. Controlling pests, including diseases and insects, through appropriate cultural and chemical methods is equally important. Using herbicides in accordance with label instructions may be necessary from time to time as a complementary measure.

To the extent that herbicide labels include references to annual bluegrass, it is usually listed as a weed to be controlled rather than as a turfgrass for which weed control is intended. Since a pesticide label is considered a legal document that limits how the herbicide may be used, the legality of using specific herbicides for controlling weeds in an annual bluegrass turf may, in some instances, be borderline, if not illegal. This situation should be addressed by herbicide manufacturers as soon as possible.

Herbicides are seldom used on annual bluegrass greens because of the high potential for phytotoxicity. Small weed infestations can be physically removed and the turf repaired, as is commonly done for ball marks. Larger infestations can be plugged out using a cup cutter; new turf is then installed from a creeping bentgrass or annual bluegrass nursery green. On tee boxes, herbicides, to the extent that they are used at all, should be selected carefully to ensure that they do not impede recovery from vegetative growth, germination of residual annual bluegrass seed, or seedling growth of overseeded turfgrasses. This precludes the use of all preemergence herbicides except siduron (Tupersan) and limits the use of postemergence herbicides to those that do not substantially reduce the turf's recuperative ability. With respect to fairways, both preemergence and postemergence herbicides may be used as long as they don't substantially reduce the stress tolerance of annual bluegrass during the summer months. Regardless of the herbicide proposed for use, always test the material on a small section of turf to ensure that it can be used safely, as the enormous genetic diversity within the annual bluegrass species can result in highly unpredictable responses.

Annual Grasses

Crabgrass (*Digitaria* sp.)

The crabgrass genus includes two species of importance in annual bluegrass turf; these are smooth crabgrass [*Digitaria ischaemum* (Schreb.) Muhl.] and large or hairy crabgrass [*Digitaria sanguinalis* (L.) Scop.]. These are plants with bunch-type growth habits and short decumbent stems that root at the nodes (Figure 3.3, see color insert). Seed heads appear as several fingerlike projections at the terminals of seed stalks. The principal difference between these species is the abundance of hairs along the leaf sheaths of *D. sanguinalis* and their absence in *D. ischaemum*.

OCCURRENCE

Smooth and hairy crabgrass are summer annuals that germinate in late spring or summer on warm, moist sites with moderate to full sunlight. The rapid tillering of crabgrasses during warm periods favorable to their growth tends to crowd out annual bluegrass and other cool-season turfgrass species. Growth slows considerably during cool weather in late summer and early fall, and plants are usually killed with the first hard frost, leaving unsightly brown patches in the turf.

MANAGEMENT

While the primary defense against invasion of annual bluegrass turf by summer annual grasses is through the maintenance of healthy and vigorous growth by annual bluegrass, some mechanical or chemical weed control may be necessary. On greens crabgrasses should be controlled primarily by mechanical means (i.e., knifing or plugging out). On tees, postemergence applications of fenoxyprop p-ethyl (Acclaim Extra) may be used to control newly germinated stands of crabgrass; however, efficacy declines as crabgrass plants mature and produce more tillers. Efficacy is also reduced under droughty conditions or when these chemicals are mixed with 2,4-D and related phenoxycarboxylic acid herbicides. Well-established crabgrass (i.e., more than four tillers) is more easily controlled with postemergence applications of quinclorac (Drive). In addition to postemergence herbicides, some preemergence herbicides may be used on fairways; however, with the exception of siduron (Tupersan), annual bluegrass may be rendered more sensitive to summer stress by spring applications of dithiopyr (Dimension), pendimethalin (Pendulum, Pre-M), and other preemergence herbicides. Also, to the extent that an annual bluegrass community is dependent on seed germination to maintain stand density and turf quality, preemergence herbicides will probably prevent new seedlings from developing as long as sufficient residues persist in the soil. Dithiopyr is unique among the preemergence herbicides in that it also provides some early postemergence activity. Where dithiopyr is applied to untillered crabgrass, or to crabgrass with no more than two tillers, satisfactory control can be achieved. A possible alternative to conventional preemergence herbicides for crabgrass control is corn gluten meal (CGM), a by-product of corn wet milling containing a series of dipeptides that inhibit mitosis in root tips. Although CGM has not been studied for crabgrass control in annual bluegrass turf, the available data suggest that it might be a safer alternative to conventional preemergence herbicides for this purpose; however, large quantities of nitrogen are also applied using this source at rates sufficient to provide crabgrass control.

Goosegrass [*Eleusine indica* (L.) Gaertn.]

Goosegrass is similar to crabgrass in appearance but is usually darker green in color (Figure 3.4, see color insert). It has a center that is a silvery color; hence, the alternative name *silver crabgrass*. Its seed heads are zipperlike in appearance.

OCCURRENCE

Goosegrass is a summer annual that begins germinating 2 to 3 weeks after crabgrass. It is usually found in compacted and poorly drained soils in warm temperate (and warmer) climates. Once germination begins, it continues until frost, whereas smooth crabgrass rarely germinates after mid-July.

MANAGEMENT

Goosegrass infestations on greens should be controlled mechanically. On tees and fairways, fenoxyprop *p*-ethyl should be applied at light rates every 2 weeks to control young populations of goosegrass germinating throughout the summer. These applications could be made in combination with fungicides where disease control is needed. Dithiopyr and pendimethalin are preemergence herbicides that are effective against goosegrass; however, their use on annual bluegrass fairways may render the turf more sensitive to summer stress.

Perennial Grasses and Sedges

Bentgrass (*Agrostis* sp.)

Although listing creeping bentgrass (*A. stolonifera* L.) or other bentgrass species as weeds in annual bluegrass turf may seem odd, golfers are sometimes observed to move the ball from a patch of prostrate-growing creeping bentgrass to a more upright stand of annual bluegrass, which often provides a better lie. Still, the incidence of bentgrass patches in annual bluegrass is usually not a cause for concern, and control measures would not normally be contemplated. Where bentgrass control in fairways is desired, it can be achieved through spot treatments with glyphosate (Roundup Pro, etc.) or glufosinate-ammonium (Finale) in late summer, when a new crop of annual bluegrass can be expected to germinate from accumulated seed in the turf.

Perennial Ryegrass (*Lolium perenne* L.)

Where perennial ryegrass and annual bluegrass occur in the same turf, textural and color differences often result in a nonuniform appearance that can significantly reduce turf quality and playability.

OCCURRENCE

Mixed stands of perennial ryegrass and annual bluegrass usually result from attempts to introduce perennial ryegrass into annual bluegrass turfs through overseeding operations and where subsequent attempts to eradicate annual bluegrass have not been successful.

MANAGEMENT

Control measures are the same as those for bentgrass.

Rough Bluegrass (*Poa trivialis* L.)

Rough bluegrass is a stoloniferous species that produces individual light green patches that can disrupt an otherwise uniform annual bluegrass fairway turf. Because of the prostrate growth of this grass at fairway height, the patches can reduce the turf's playability. During summer conditions it tends to thin and go off-color, further disrupting its appearance and playability.

OCCURRENCE

Rough bluegrass is adapted to moist, fertile soils and grows aggressively during cool wet weather, especially on moderately shaded sites.

MANAGEMENT

Control measures are the same as those for bentgrass.

Yellow Nutsedge (*Cyperus esculentus* L.)

Yellow nutsedge is a perennial that reproduces by seed, rhizomes, and small hard tubers called *nutlets*. It is distinguished from grasses by its triangular stems and three-ranked leaves. The nutlets may persist in the soil for several years, ensuring regeneration of the plants when conditions are favorable.

OCCURRENCE

Yellow nutsedge occurs on moist sites, especially where drainage is poor. Its shoots first appear in mid to late spring following germination of the nutlets. Vigorous growth in the summer can result in rapid population increases. Aerial shoots disappear in late fall, followed by overwintering of the nutlets. Once a turf has become infested with yellow nutsedge, reinfestation is almost assured for several succeeding years, due to the presence and persistence of nutlets in the soil.

MANAGEMENT

In addition to improving drainage and other conditions to support healthy turfgrass growth, bentazon (Basagran, Lescogran) should be used to kill new plants before they produce a new crop of nutlets. Halosulfuron (Manage) can provide even more effective control, but annual bluegrass may be severely damaged by this herbicide.

Broadleaf Weeds

White Clover (*Trifolium repens* L.)

White clover is a creeping perennial that competes aggressively with established turfgrasses. It has a stout taproot and branched stolons and is identified by its three short-stalked leaflets and globular white flowers (Figure 3.5, see color insert).

OCCURRENCE

Although white clover grows especially well under moist conditions and low soil fertility, its pervasive incidence in intensively cultured turfs suggests that it is adapted to a wide range of environmental and cultural conditions, even at mowing heights employed on greens.

MANAGEMENT

White clover can be controlled with selected phenoxycarboxylic acid (mecoprop, dichloroprop), pyridinecarboxylic acid (triclopyr, clopyralid), quinolinecarboxylic acid (quinclorac), benzoic acid (dicamba), and aryltriazolinone (carfentrazone) herbicides applied in combinations or, in some cases, individually (Table 3.2). Because of the influence of genotype and cultural intensity on the sensitivity of annual bluegrass to these herbicides, however, careful testing should be done before selecting the herbicides or herbicide combinations that should be used on annual bluegrass turfs. For example, the combination of tryclopyr and clopyralid, available commercially as Confront, can be especially injurious to annual bluegrass under certain application conditions (Figure 3.6, see color insert).

TABLE 3.2
Guide to Controlling Weeds of Annual Bluegrass Turf

Herbicide	Application Characteristics		Turf Type		Annual Grasses		Perennial Grasses and Sedges				Broadleaf Weeds		
	Preemergence/ Postemergence	Selective/ Nonselective	Greens	Fairways	Crabgrass	Goosegrass	Creeping Bentgrass	Perennial Ryegrass	Rough Bluegrass	Yellow Nutsedge	White Clover	Mouse-Ear Chickweed	Pearlwort
Bentazon	Post	Sel.		×						×			
Carfentrazone, 2,4-D, mecoprop, dicamba	Post	Sel.		×							×	×	
Carfentrazone, MCPA, mecoprop, dicamba	Post	Sel.		×							×	×	
Clopyralid	Post	Sel.		×							×		
Corn gluten	Pre	Sel.			×								
2,4-D, dicamba	Post	Sel.									×	×	
2,4-D, dichloroprop	Post	Sel.									×	×	
2,4-D, dichloroprop, dicamba	Post	Sel.									×	×	
2,4-D, mecoprop	Post	Sel.									×	×	
2,4-D, mecoprop, dicamba	Post	Sel.		×							×	×	
2,4-D, mecoprop, dichloroprop											×	×	
Dicamba	Post	Sel.		×							×	×	
Dithiopyr	Pre[a]			×	×	×							
Fenoxyprop p-ethyl	Post	Sel.		×	×								
Glufosinate-ammonium	Post	Non.					×	×	×				
Glyphosate	Post	Non.					×	×	×				
Halosulfuron	Post	Sel.								×			
Mecoprop	Post	Sel.									×	×	×
MCPA, mecoprop, dicamba	Post	Sel.									×	×	
MCPA, mecoprop, dichloroprop	Post	Sel.	×	×							×	×	
Pendimethalin	Pre			×	×	×							
Quinclorac	Post	Sel.		×	×						×	×	
Siduron	Pre			×	×								

[a]Dithiopyr also has early postemergence activity.

Mouse-Ear Chickweed (*Cerastium vulgatum* L.)

Mouse-ear chickweed is a perennial that reproduces mainly by seed but also by stolons. It is identified by its small pubescent dark green leaves and dense growth habit (Figure 3.7, see color insert).

OCCURRENCE

The presence of mouse-ear chickweed is indicative of moist, compacted soils. It can infest annual bluegrass greens, tees, and fairways, especially where disease or insect damage provide infestation windows into these turfs.

MANAGEMENT

Control measures are the same as for white clover.

Pearlwort (*Sagina procumbens* L.)

Pearlwort is a winter annual or perennial that reproduces by both seed and stolons to form dense patches in greens and other intensively cultured turfs (Figure 3.8, see color insert). Because its leaves are grasslike in appearance, it is often confused with annual bluegrass. Its flowers are tiny, with white petals and four longer sepals; flowering occurs from late spring to first frost in the fall.

OCCURRENCE

Pearlwort occurs in cool, wet, poorly drained soils and is well adapted to close mowing.

MANAGEMENT

Control measures are similar to those for white clover, but generally less effective.

Moss

Mosses encompass many species of threadlike, branched, primitive plants that spread by spores. They do not produce true roots; instead, filamentous structures, called rhizoids, absorb water from the soil but do not provide anchorage.

OCCURRENCE

Mosses are most likely to occur in greens and tees on moist shaded sites; however, they can quickly populate both shaded and sunny sites where thinning of the stand provides infestation windows into

FIGURE 3.1 ■ *Seed head suppression by mefluidide (Embark) on annual bluegrass plot.*

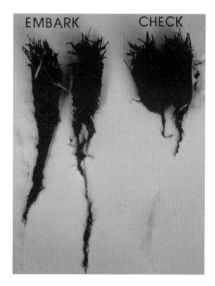

FIGURE 3.2 ■ *Annual bluegrass root response from mefluidide (Embark) treatment (left) compared with the control plants (right).*

FIGURE 3.3 ■ *Crabgrass emergence in annual bluegrass turf. (Photo courtesy of Peter Landschoot, Penn State University.)*

FIGURE 3.4 ■ *Goosegrass emergence in annual bluegrass turf.*

FIGURE 3.5 ■ *White clover in annual bluegrass turf. (Photo courtesy of Thomas Watschke, Penn State University.)*

FIGURE 3.6 ■ *Phytotoxicity from triclopyr and clopyralid (Confront) herbicide application to annual bluegrass turf. (Photo courtesy of Peter Landschoot, Penn State University.)*

FIGURE 3.7 ■ *Mouse-ear chickweed in annual bluegrass turf.*

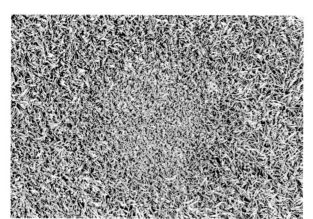

FIGURE 3.8 ■ *Pearlwort in annual bluegrass green. (Photo courtesy of Peter Landschoot, Penn State University.)*

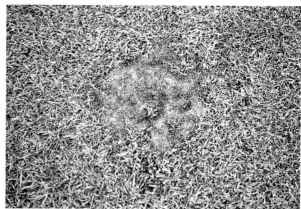

FIGURE 3.9 ■ *Moss in annual bluegrass green. (Photo courtesy of Peter Landschoot, Penn State University.)*

FIGURE 3.10 ■ *Foliar anthracnose disease in annual bluegrass turf.*

FIGURE 3.11 ■ *Crown rotting anthracnose in annual bluegrass green.*

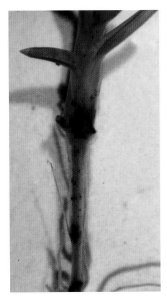

FIGURE 3.12 ■ *Crown rotting anthracnose infection of annual bluegrass crown.*

FIGURE 3.13 ■ *Patches of creeping bentgrass in voids resulting from summer patch disease in annual bluegrass turf.*

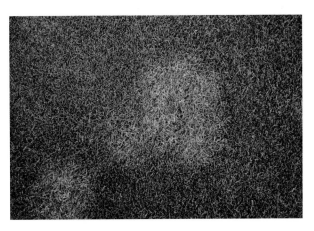

FIGURE 3.14 ■ *Summer patch disease in annual bluegrass fairway.*

FIGURE 3.15 ▨ *Summer patch disease symptoms in annual bluegrass fairway.*

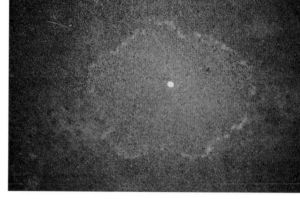

FIGURE 3.16 ▨ *Patch of creeping bentgrass in void resulting from summer patch disease in annual bluegrass turf.*

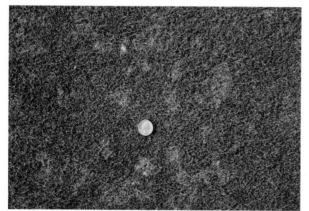

FIGURE 3.17 ▨ *Dollar spot disease symptoms in annual bluegrass turf.*

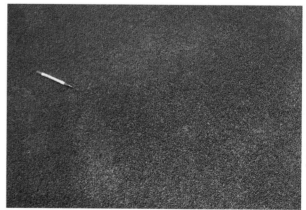

FIGURE 3.18 ▨ *Brown patch disease in annual bluegrass turf.*

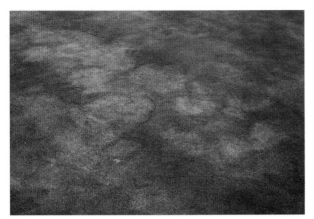

FIGURE 3.19 ■ *Brown patch disease symptoms in annual bluegrass turf.*

FIGURE 3.20 ■ Pythium *blight disease in annual bluegrass turf.*

FIGURE 3.21 ■ *Microdochium patch (pink snow mold) disease in annual bluegrass turf.*

FIGURE 3.22 ■ *Typhula blight (gray snow mold) disease in annual bluegrass turf.*

FIGURE 3.23 ■ *Black turfgrass* ataenius *damage to annual bluegrass turf.*

FIGURE 3.24 ■ *Black turfgrass* ataenius *adult. (Photo courtesy of David Smitely, Michigan State University.)*

FIGURE 3.25 ■ *Black turfgrass* ataenius *grubs.*

FIGURE 3.26 ■ *Turf damage from large animals feeding on Japanese beetle grubs. (Photo courtesy of David Smitely, Michigan State University.)*

FIGURE 3.27 ■ *Japanese beetle damage to annual bluegrass turf. (Photo courtesy of David Smitely, Michigan State University.)*

FIGURE 3.28 ■ *Japanese beetle adult. (Photo courtesy of David Smitely, Michigan State University.)*

FIGURE 3.29 ■ *Japanese beetle grub. (Photo courtesy of David Smitely, Michigan State University.)*

FIGURE 3.30 ■ *Annual bluegrass weevil damage on green and collar. (Photo courtesy of James Snow, USGA Green Section.)*

Figure 3.31 ■ *Annual bluegrass weevil damage to left side of fairway (right side renovated). (Photo courtesy of James Snow, USGA Green Section.)*

FIGURE 3.32 ■ *Annual bluegrass weevil adults feeding on grass plant. (Photo courtesy of James Snow, USGA Green Section.)*

FIGURE 3.33 ■ *Annual bluegrass weevil adult (left) and grub (right). (Photo courtesy of James Snow, USGA Green Section.)*

FIGURE 3.34 ■ *Black cutworm damage on green.*

FIGURE 3.35 ■ *Black cutworm larva.*

the turf. The occurrence of algae can sometimes predispose a turf to moss invasion. As moss density increases to form dense mats, all turfgrass plants may be crowded out (Figure 3.9, see color insert).

MANAGEMENT

Conditions associated with the deterioration of a turf and subsequent moss infestation should be corrected. Excessive surface moisture can be reduced by improving air circulation, light exposure, and drainage, and reducing irrigation. Healthy turfgrass growth can be encouraged by raising the mowing height; avoiding excessive nitrogen fertilization while ensuring that adequate nitrogen, as well as potassium, are available; and applying lime to raise the soil pH to an optimum level. Spiking, vertical mowing, and topdressing can be performed to break up and remove moss mats. Chemical control is erratic, especially if conditions favoring moss infestations are not corrected. Some success has been reported from multiple applications of various materials, including HO_2 (fatty acid salts), ferrous and ferric sulfates, and copper hydroxide ± mancozeb. Great care must be taken to ensure that unacceptable phytotoxcity to the turf is avoided, as all of these materials can cause injury.

DISEASES

Anthracnose: Foliar and Crown Rotting

Pathogen: *Colletotrichum graminicola* (Ces) Wils (syn. *C. cereale* Manns).

Foliar Anthracnose

Foliar anthracnose is a disease that occurs on annual bluegrass during warm weather. A predictive model developed by Danneberger et al. (1984) showed that nighttime temperatures had to remain above 68°F (20°C), with continuous leaf wetness for 8 hours or more, and daytime temperature had to exceed 86°F (30°C) for three consecutive days. Later, moisture stress was also shown to be important in the development of foliar anthracnose (Danneberger et al., 1995). Infected greens or fairways normally take on a bronze appearance, with a general thinning of the turf (Figure 3.10, see color insert). If individual leaves are examined, the fruiting bodies of *C. graminicola* can be observed on the foliage. These spore-containing fruiting bodies, called *acervuli*, are black with little spines, called *setae*. The disease can spread rapidly, destroying large areas of annual bluegrass in a single evening. In the past, dramatic losses of annual bluegrass in summer were often attributed to wilting and subsequent death from high-temperature stress; however, wilted annual bluegrass turns blue or purple, not bronze.

Crown Rotting Anthracnose

Crown rotting anthracnose (CRA), on the other hand, occurs over a wide range of temperatures. As its occurrence can immediately follow snowmelt, it is believed that the disease can actually occur under snow cover. It can also be a problem during cool, wet weather in spring and fall, as well as in warm, wet summer weather. Such broad adaptation to a wide temperature range suggests that different strains of *C. graminicola* are causing the disease. Pathogen variation among isolates of *C. graminicola* with the capacity to attack annual bluegrass and creeping bentgrass were reported by Blackman et al. (1999) and Horvath (1999).

The one constant that has been observed in outbreaks of CRA is saturated soils, normally caused by heavy rainfall but also by excessive irrigation. Saturated soils following snowmelt can also be a factor in the outbreak of CRA. Symptoms first appear as bronze- to yellow-colored spots in the turf, about the size of a dime, reflecting infection of the crowns of individual plants (Figure 3.11, see color insert). As the disease spreads to adjacent plants, the spots become larger. Entire annual bluegrass greens can be destroyed in a short period of time. If the strain of *C. graminicola* can only infect annual bluegrass, patches of healthy creeping bentgrass will be seen interspersed within an otherwise severely diseased turf. Individual plants of annual bluegrass can be removed, washed, and examined with a hand lens (Figure 3.12, see color insert) to distinguish CRA from other diseases (or physiological stresses causing the annual bluegrass to go off color). Elongated crowns of infected plants appear black when examined with a hand lens; as the infection may occur on only one side, it is important to examine all sides of the crown. Under a dissecting microscope, the acervuli and setae of the pathogen are clearly visible.

Annual Bluegrass Culture

Many "greens-type" annual bluegrasses are especially susceptible to CRA and summer patch; these diseases are more difficult to
control on this type than on other commonly occurring types of
annual bluegrass.

MANAGEMENT: CULTURAL

The severity of foliar anthracnose can be reduced by optimum levels
of nitrogen fertility, which also appear to enhance the efficacy of fungicides in controlling the disease. Nitrogen fertility will also reduce
the severity of CRA.

MANAGEMENT: CHEMICAL

Foliar anthracnose can be controlled by many fungicides, including the
benzimidazoles (e.g., thiophanate methyl), the demethylation inhibitors
(DMIs, e.g., fenarimol, myclobutanil, propiconazol, and triadimefon),
and the Qo1 (formerly, strobularin) fungicides (e.g., azoxystrobin,
trifloxystrobin). They work well when applied either curatively or preventively.

Controlling CRA is a little more complex. The benzimidazoles
have to be applied at relatively high rates and drenched in to be effective; the demethylation inhibitors need to be applied with at least
5 gallons of water per 1000 ft^2 (20 L per 100 m^2) to be effective,
whereas azoxystrobin can be applied at lower spray volumes and
does not need to be drenched in to be effective.

Patch Diseases

Summer Patch

Pathogen: *Magnathae poae* Landschoot & Jackson.

SYMPTOMS

Summer patch symptoms are normally seen in the summer months
when warm temperatures are followed by heavy rains or excessive
irrigation. The disease first appears as yellow- to bronze-colored
patches. The circular or irregularly shaped patches vary from 6 to 12
in. (15 to 30 cm) in diameter (Figures 3.13, 3.14, and 3.15, see color
insert). If the disease persists, the plants in these spots will either die
or go dormant. With the return of cool weather, some of the patches
recover very quickly, suggesting that some of the infected annual

bluegrass plants go dormant rather than die. If summer patch occurs on annual bluegrass in mixed swards with creeping bentgrass, pure stands of creeping bentgrass will dominate the patches as the summer patch removes annual bluegrass from the sward (Figures 3.13 and 3.16, see color insert). If the infected swards are pure annual bluegrass, bare soil will become evident where summer patch has eliminated the annual bluegrass.

MANAGEMENT: CULTURAL

As with most patch diseases, adequate levels of nitrogen fertility reduce the severity of summer patch. Studies at Michigan State University have shown that 0.5 lb N per 1000 ft^2 (0.25 kg N per 100 m^2) applied during June, July, and August will help reduce the severity of summer patch (Vargas, 1994). In warmer climates similar applications should be made in May and September as well. The addition of nitrogen also improves the efficacy of fungicides in controlling this disease. Since poor drainage is associated with greater disease severity, light and frequent irrigation may be helpful in reducing this problem, while effectively alleviating moisture stress.

MANAGEMENT: CHEMICAL

There is a simple method for determining when fungicides should be applied for controlling summer patch; it consists of taking the soil temperature at a soil depth of 2 in. (5 cm) each afternoon between 1:00 and 4:00 P.M. When the soil temperature reaches 65°F (18°C) and 75°F (24°C), DMI or Qol fungicides should be applied for effective preventive control.

Once summer patch has occurred it is much more difficult to control because of destruction of the roots, and in some cases the crowns, of annual bluegrass plants. The best curative treatment is with thiophanate methyl applied at high dosage rates and drenched into the root zone.

Necrotic Ring Spot

Pathogen: *Leptosphaeria korrae* J. C. Walker & A. M. Sm.

OCCURRENCE

Necrotic ring spot is becoming an important disease, particularly on annual bluegrass greens. The disease becomes active in the late summer and fall. The symptoms are often confused with yellow patch, which also occurs at this time of year. Severe turf loss can occur if fungicides are not applied. Dead patches of turf will be present the following spring and recovery will be slow. Spring infections can occur and can also cause severe turf loss, especially with prolonged cool weather.

SYMPTOMS

The disease first appears as small patches 6 to 12 in. (15 to 30 cm) in diameter. When *L. korrae* is actively attacking annual bluegrass plants in the fall, the disease appears as yellow patches. Infected plants eventually die, becoming brown to straw colored. When the green breaks dormancy in the spring, the patches are evident as depressions, which interfere with putting.

MANAGEMENT: CULTURAL

Little research has been done on this disease in annual bluegrass. Based on what we know from research on necrotic ring spot on Kentucky bluegrass, it would seem logical to assume that nitrogen will help reduce the severity of the disease. Also, optimizing nitrogen fertility has been shown to reduce the severity of similar cool-season patch diseases, such as summer patch and take-all patch.

MANAGEMENT: CHEMICAL

There has been no published research on controlling necrotic ring spot in annual bluegrass. If we extrapolate from the research done on necrotic ring spot on Kentucky bluegrass and the other patch diseases, the DMI fungicides (e.g., propiconazole, fenarimol, and myclobutanil) should work if applied before symptoms occur, azoxystrobin should control the disease if applied when symptoms first appear, and thiophanate methyl should work best once the disease is present. For the curative fungicide treatments to be effective, however, they must be applied before the pathogen has destroyed the plant's crown.

Dollar Spot

Pathogen: *Rutstremia flocossum,* Powell and Vargas [formerly *Sclerotinia homoeocarpa* F.T. Bennett].

Dollar spot is an unsightly disease of annual bluegrass. While large portions of greens, tees, and fairways can be damaged during severe outbreaks of the disease, they normally recover with the development of cool fall weather. This is often what is observed on fairways of low-budget public golf courses where the cost of spraying fairways is prohibitive.

SYMPTOMS

Dollar spot appears as round bleached-out spots ranging from the size of a quarter to that of a silver dollar (Figure 3.17, see color insert). The spots tend to have a silver cast to them; thus, the name *dollar spot*. The spots appear as sunken areas in the turf. Individual spots may coalesce, giving large areas of turf a silver cast. In the early morning while the grass is still wet from dew, grayish-white fluffy mycelium of the pathogen may be present.

Dollar spot symptoms on individual annual bluegrass blades appear as bleached-out lesions that usually extend across the entire width of the blade. The characteristic reddish-brown bands present at the outer edges of the leaf lesions in bentgrasses, Kentucky bluegrass, fine-leaf fescue, zoysiagrass, and bermudagrass are absent in annual bluegrass.

OCCURRENCE

Dollar spot occurs at temperatures between 60 and 90°F (16 and 32°C). Over 20 vegetatively compatible groups of the pathogen have been identified. These have been shown to occur at different times during the growing season, depending on temperature. High humidity and the occurrence of guttation fluid are important in the development of the disease.

MANAGEMENT: CULTURAL

The severity of dollar spot disease in annual bluegrass can be reduced by supplying sufficient amounts of nitrogen. Frequent light applications of nitrogen are best, both for managing the disease and for general growth of the grass plant, especially during warm weather. Higher nitrogen application rates can be used in the cooler weather of late summer or early fall when diseases such as brown patch and *Pythium* blight are no longer of concern.

Removing the dew (specifically, the guttation fluid) to prevent dollar spot is a common practice on greens. It typically involves poling the green with a bamboo pole, dragging a hose over the area, or applying irrigation water to remove the dew from the leaves and wash it into the turf. Removing the guttation fluid with a hose or through irrigation is also practiced on fairways. The latter practice may seem to defeat the purpose, since you are trying to dry off the green, but what you really want to do is remove or dilute the guttation water. Guttation fluid is rich in carbohydrates and amino acids that are exuded from the tip of the grass blade through structures called *hydothodes* when turgor pressure builds up in the plant. This fluid supplies a nutrient-rich medium that supports the growth of the dollar spot fungus as it spreads from leaf to leaf. Therefore, anything that will remove guttation water, such as diluting it with irrigation water or breaking up the droplets so that the foliage will dry faster, can help reduce the severity of the disease.

MANAGEMENT: GENETIC

Annual bluegrass is such a diverse species that there may be populations resistant to *R. floccosum* that someday might be selected and developed as commercial cultivars of this species; however, resistance to dollar spot in annual bluegrass has not been reported or observed.

MANAGEMENT: BIOLOGICAL

Nelsen and Craft (1991) have demonstrated suppression of dollar spot under field conditions with both composted materials (e.g., Ringers Compost Plus) and a bacterium called *Enterobacter cloacae*. Goodman and Burpee (1991) were able to suppress dollar spot in the greenhouse with a fungus called *Fusarium heterosporum*. During years of heavy infections, however, fungicide treatments will be necessary to obtain satisfactory control.

In recent work at Michigan State University, effective control of dollar spot in annual bluegrass maintained as fairway turf was demonstrated with *Pseudomonas aureofaciens* applied five times a week at 2×10^7 colony-forming units (CFU)/cm^2.

MANAGEMENT: CHEMICAL

Many contact and systemic fungicides can manage dollar spot (Table 3.3). Resistance to the benzimidazoles, dicarboximides, and DMI fungicides by *R. flocossum* has been reported for annual bluegrass (Golb, 1995; Golembieski et al., 1995). Resistance to the dicarboximide and DMI fungicides occurs initially as a shortening of the

TABLE 3.3
Guide to Controlling Annual Bluegrass Diseases

Fungicide	Diseases											
	Algae	Anthracnose	Brown Patch	Dollar Spot	Fairy Rings	Microdocium Patch	Necrotic Ring Spot	Pythium Blight	Summer Patch[a]	Typhula Blight[b]	Yellow Patch	Yellow Tufts
Azoxystrobin		×	×		×[c]	×	×		×	×	×	
Chloroneb								×				
Chlorothalonil	×		×	×		×				×	×	
Etridiazole								×				
Fenarimol		×		×		×	×		×	×		
Flutolanil			×		×[c]						×	
Fosetyl-Al		×						×				
Iprodione			×	×		×				×	×	
Mancozeb	×		×								×	
Mefenoxam								×				×
Myclobutanil		×		×		×	×			×		
PCNB										×		
Propiconazole		×		×		×	×		×	×		
Thiophanate-methyl		×						×	×			
Triadimefon		×		×		×	×		×	×		
Trifluxystrobin		×				×			×	×	×	
Vinclozolin			×	×		×				×	×	

[a]Mostly preventive; use only thiohanate-methyl for curative control after symptoms appear.
[b]Use half rate of PCNB and chlorothalonil; combine with one of the other fungicides.
[c]Works on some but not all fairy rings.

longevity of control; continued use of these products will eventually lead to complete lack of control. Since strains of *R. flocossum* with resistance to these fungicides have been reported; alternating or combining them in a preventive fungicide-application program will do little to delay or prevent resistance. For a more detailed discussion of the subject, see Vargas (1994).

Brown Patch (*Rhizoctonia* Blight)

Pathogen: *Rhizoctonia solani* Kuhn.

Brown patch is a disease of many cool- and warm-season grasses, including annual bluegrass. The pathogen that causes brown patch, *R. solani,* is made up of several anastomosis groups. The one that most commonly occurs on annual bluegrass is AgA1A. The disease can cause considerable damage to annual bluegrass turfs, especially in the warmer regions where annual bluegrass is maintained. Recovery is often slow because the high temperatures that favor the disease do not favor recovery of surviving plants or the development of new plants from the annual bluegrass seed reservoir in the soil.

SYMPTOMS

The disease occurs in the turf as circular patches, from a few inches up to several feet in diameter (Figures 3.18 and 3.19, see color insert). The infected leaves first appear water-soaked and dark, eventually turning dark brown. When the humidity is high, a "smoke ring" consisting of the fungal mycelium is sometimes observed surrounding the outer margins of the diseased area, especially in the early morning hours. This typically disappears by midmorning as the foliage dries.

OCCURRENCE

R. solani survives adverse periods as sclerotia or as mycelium in plant debris. It can also survive as a saprophyte in the thatch. When the soil temperature rises above 60°F (16°C) in spring, the sclerotia begin to germinate and the fungus grows saprophytically. *R. solani* is basically a weak parasite that causes only mild damage until daytime temperatures reach approximately 86°F (30°C) with high humidity and nighttime temperatures exceeding 70°F (21°C). At low temperatures *R. solani* grows as a saprophyte or causes minute infections that do not seriously damage healthy grass plants; however, with heat stress or high-temperature growth stoppage of annual bluegrass, fungal infection is favored, and serious disease incidences can occur. As with most fungi, growth occurs in a circular pattern. Under highly favorable conditions, large infected patches of annual bluegrass will appear to develop overnight; however, these are the result of saprophytic fungal growth in the soil or thatch for many days prior to pathogenic infection.

MANAGEMENT: CULTURAL

High rates of nitrogen fertilizer applied during or just prior to the onset of hot, humid weather can substantially increase the severity of the disease. Under these conditions, nitrogen applications, to the extent that they are needed at all, should be limited to 0.5 lb per 1000 ft^2 (0.25 kg N per 100 m^2) per month. Adequate levels of phosphorus and potassium should always be maintained, based on soil test results. As with dollar spot, removal of the dew (specifically, guttation water) in the early morning hours will help reduce disease severity.

MANAGEMENT: GENETIC

Whereas annual bluegrass is certainly susceptible to brown patch, it is not as severely affected by this disease as are colonial bentgrass, perennial ryegrass, and tall fescue, which are all highly susceptible. Creeping bentgrass, especially the new high-density Penn A- and G-series cultivars, are also somewhat more susceptible to brown patch disease than is annual bluegrass.

MANAGEMENT: CHEMICAL

There are both contact and systemic fungicides available for the management of brown patch on annual bluegrass. Because infection takes place long before symptoms are evident, large areas of turf can suddenly appear severely diseased. If not treated immediately, especially in sustained hot and humid weather, a considerable amount of grass may quickly be lost. Since recovery may not take place until cool weather returns, a preventive fungicide program is suggested.

The contact fungicide chlorothalonil has been used for many years to manage brown patch. It is effective for about 10 days under normal disease pressure. Various formulations of maneb and mancozeb have also been used; these are effective for about 7 days. Brown patch can be managed effectively by systemic fungicides: flutolanil will provide 14 to 21 days of control, and azoxystrobin or trifluxystrobin 21 to 28 days, under normal disease pressure.

Yellow Patch

Pathogen: *Rhizoctonia cerealis,* Van derHoeven.

Yellow patch can be a serious disease of annual bluegrass greens, but it tends to be more unsightly than destructive.

SYMPTOMS

The disease appears as pale yellow more-or-less circular patches. The symptoms are similar to those of summer patch, necrotic ring spot, and superficial fairy ring, and may be confused with these diseases. Yellow patch can easily be distinguished from the others by microscopic examination. Turfgrass plants infected by *R. cerealis* have an abundance of brown mycelium under the leaf sheath.

OCCURRENCE

Yellow patch is a problem primarily in the cool, wet weather of spring or early fall. It can occur on all types of annual bluegrass turfs; however, it is usually a concern only when it occurs on greens.

MANAGEMENT: CHEMICAL

Both contact and systemic fungicides are available for the management of yellow patch on annual bluegrass. Yellow patch is normally controlled on a curative basis. Under normal disease pressure, control will normally last about 10 days from chlorothalonil; 14 to 21 days from iprodione or vinclozolin; and 21 to 28 days from flutolanil, azoxystrobin, or trifloxystrobin.

Pythium Blight (Grease Spot, Cottony Blight)

Pathogen: *Pythium aphanidermatum* (Edson)
Fitzpatrick (syn. *butleri* subrm.).

Pythium blight can be devastating on annual bluegrass when temperature and humidity are high. Although it usually doesn't destroy large areas of turf overnight as commonly thought, *Pythium* blight can advance fairly quickly when environmental conditions are favorable.

SYMPTOMS

Pythium blight first appears as circular reddish-brown spots in the turf, ranging from 1 to 3 in. (2.5 to 7.5 cm) in diameter (Figure 3.20, see color insert). Infected leaf blades appear water soaked and dark, and may feel slimy when first observed in the morning. The blades shrivel and turn reddish brown as they dry. Active purplish-gray mycelium can be seen in the outer margins of the spots as long as the foliage remains wet.

The infected grass plants collapse quickly. If the temperature and humidity remain high, the spots may coalesce, and large areas of turf can be affected. As *P. aphanidermatum* is a water mold, it can be spread by surface water movement and mower traffic on wet turf. The pattern of disease symptoms often reflects the pattern of the pathogen's movement across the turf.

OCCURRENCE

Like *Rhizoctonia* and *Colletotrichum, Pythium* is a good saprophyte. It is usually present in the thatch, soil, or both, and simply requires favorable environmental conditions to become pathogenic. Since it can survive as a saprophyte in the soil for many years without becoming pathogenic, it can cause disease in marginal areas where environmental conditions for *Pythium* blight occur only once every four or five years.

MANAGEMENT: CULTURAL

Good soil drainage is essential for effective management of *Pythium* blight. Annual bluegrass growing in poorly drained or compacted soils where water tends to stand has more severe outbreaks of *Pythium* blight. Intensive irrigation will tend to increase the severity of the disease. Improving drainage can help manage *Pythium* blight. Annual bluegrass turfs should not be watered until the foliage is completely dry during *Pythium* blight outbreaks. Light midday irrigation allows the turf to dry before nightfall and thus helps reduce disease pressure. Nighttime irrigation should be avoided altogether. There is, however, no substitute for good soil drainage. In cool regions where *Pythium* blight is a not a major problem, the disease usually occurs only in poorly drained areas. Improving air circulation also helps to manage this disease.

High nitrogen levels cause lush growth and make *Pythium* blight worse. No special program of nitrogen fertilization is necessary, since low-to-moderate nitrogen is normally recommended for annual bluegrass during hot, humid weather.

MANAGEMENT: GENETIC

The perennial ryegrasses are the most susceptible to *Pythium* blight, followed by the turf-type tall fescues and annual bluegrass. The creeping bentgrasses are not as susceptible to *Pythium* blight as is annual bluegrass.

MANAGEMENT: CHEMICAL

There are many good fungicides for the control of *Pythium* blight, such as the contact fungicides chloroneb and ethazole, which normally have a 5- to 7-day residual, and the systemic fungicides propamocarb, metalaxyl, and fosetyl-aluminum, which normally have a 10- to 14-day residual when disease pressure is heavy. All have good curative as well as preventive activity except fosetyl-aluminum, which only works preventively.

Snow Molds

Microdochium Patch (Pink Snow Mold)

Pathogen: *Microdochium nivale* (Fr.) Samuels & 1. C. Hallett (syn. *Fusarium nivale* Ces. ex Berl. & Voglino).

OCCURRENCE

Annual bluegrass is highly susceptible to *Microdochium* patch. It is not uncommon to see *Microdochium* patch occurring selectively on annual bluegrass in mixed stands with creeping bentgrass. *Microdochium* patch is considered one of the most important diseases of annual bluegrass in the Pacific northwestern United States and northwestern Europe, where temperate-oceanic climates prevail. The reason that *Microdochium* patch is such an important disease in these areas is because it develops during extended periods of cool, wet weather, which persists for much of the growing season in these locations. *Microdochium nivale* can survive as mycelium and spores in the thatch and will grow actively on the grass residue. Infection can take place when the temperatures are below

60°F (16°C), but the disease develops most rapidly at temperatures between 60 and 70°F (16 to 21°C).

SYMPTOMS

Microdochium patch appears as reddish-brown spots in annual bluegrass turf (Figure 3.21, see color insert). The spots normally range in diameter from less than 1 in. (2.5 cm) to about 8 in. (20 cm). Heavy rains or mowing equipment can transport fungal spores across the turf, causing streak-shaped disease symptoms similar to those occurring with *Pythium* blight; thus, it is often confused with *Pythium* blight despite the fact that these two diseases occur under entirely different sets of environmental conditions.

When *Microdochium* patch occurs under snow cover, the circular spots usually range from 2 in. to 2 ft (5.0 to 60 cm) in diameter and are tan to pinkish gray in color. Shortly after the snow has melted, the pink mycelium of the fungus may be seen at the advancing edge of the spot; hence the common name *pink snow mold*; however, *Microdochium* patch can also develop without snow cover.

MANAGEMENT: CULTURAL

Excessive nitrogen fertilization causes lush growth going into the snow-mold season and will increase the turf's susceptibility to *Microdochium* patch and make effective management with fungicides more difficult.

MANAGEMENT: CHEMICAL

There are a few contact fungicides that can be used to manage *Microdochium* patch where snow cover is absent or not persistent. Several applications will be necessary to provide control. The most commonly used fungicide is mancozeb, although chlorothalonil is also used. The systemic fungicides, including the benzimidazole, dicarboximide, DMI, and Qol fungicides, are also used. Resistance to the benzimidazole and dicarboximide fungicides by *M. nivale* has been reported in the Pacific Northwest, where successive applications are made through most of the year. In areas where *Microdochium* patch occurs under continuous snow cover so that successive fungicide applications cannot be made, PCNB alone or in combination with some of the above-mentioned fungicides is the preferred treatment for *Microdochium* patch.

Typhula Blight (Gray Snow Mold)

Pathogens: *Typhula incarnata* Lasch ex Fr.
(syn. *Typhula itoana* Imai), *Typhula ishikariensis* Imai.

Typhula blight can cause disease on annual bluegrass where snow cover remains on the ground for three or more months; however, the disease is more problematic on creeping bentgrass and perennial ryegrass than on annual bluegrass. Although *Typhula* blight can occur simultaneously with *Microdochium* patch on annual bluegrass, its range does not extend as far south (in the northern hemisphere) as that of *Microdochium* patch. Unlike *Microdochium* patch, which occurs with or without snow cover, *Typhula* blight does require some type of cover, usually by snow, but also by leaves, straw mulch, or desiccation blankets, to develop.

SYMPTOMS

At temperatures between 30 and 55°F (−1 to 13°C), the *Typhula* fungus grows and infects. As the snow melts, circular grayish or straw-colored to dark brown infection centers appear in the turf. The spots range from 3 to 24 in. (8 to 60 cm) in diameter, but most are between 6 and 12 in. (15 to 30 cm) across (Figure 3.22, see color insert). Immediately after the snow melts, the grayish-white fungal mycelium can be seen, especially at the outer margins of the spots. The disease gets its common name, gray snow mold, from the color of the mycelium. *Typhula* blight is worse in winters when the snow falls on unfrozen turf, or on turf that has not been hardened off by frost. When snow falls on frozen ground, the disease often develops in the spring after the snow begins to melt.

The two species can be separated easily when viewed shortly after snowmelt. *T. incarnata* produces large rust-colored sclerotia in infected turf, whereas *T. ishikariensis* produces small black-colored sclerotia, which create the appearance that the turf has been sprinkled with pepper.

OCCURRENCE

The *Typhula* fungi oversummer as sclerotia in the thatch and soil, where they survive unfavorable conditions. Fungicides that may be part of a summer disease control program have no effect on these resting structures. Under cool, wet fall conditions and in the presence of ultraviolet light, the sclerotia swell and germinate, producing pink club-shaped sphorophores from which basidia and basidiospores arise. The basidiospores are carried by the wind to other locations, including areas where the disease was eradicated the preceding season. The spores germinate and infect the grass plants under snow or other suitable cover. The sclerotia may germinate, form mycelium, and cause infection.

MANAGEMENT: CULTURAL

It is important that annual bluegrass not be lush going into the winter; if it is, *Typhula* blight will be much worse. It is very difficult to give a date for the last application of nitrogen to actively growing turfgrass, as dates for the first lasting snowfall vary so much from year to year. Depending on the area, the last nitrogen application should be sometime between mid-August and mid-September. This is not to be confused with dormant nitrogen feeding; that is, applying nitrogen after top growth has stopped. Dormant feedings promote early greenup in the spring and quick recovery of turf damaged by snow mold. Fungicides should always be applied to turf receiving dormant nitrogen feedings.

MANAGEMENT: BIOLOGICAL

Burpee et al. (1987) have been able to manage this disease biologically with a nonpathogenic species of *Typhula* called *Typhula phacorrhiza*. They were able to show that if nonpathogenic *T. phacorrhiza* could colonize the turf first, infection by the pathogenic *T. incarnata* and *T. ishikariensis* could be prevented. Subsequent studies in Wisconsin have shown some strains of *T. phacorrhiza* to be pathogenic and capable of causing snow mold. These suggest that more studies are needed with *T. pacorrhiza* before it is used as a biological control for *Typhula* blight.

MANAGEMENT: CHEMICAL

PCNB fungicides alone or in combination with chlorothalonil and/or the benzimidazoles or dicarboximides, and to a lesser degree in combination with the DMI or stroblarin fungicides, can provide effective control of *Typhula* blight. The DMI fungicides, including fenarimol, triadimefon, and propiconazole, are labeled for snow mold, and in the eastern United States, where only *T. incarnata* occurs, they are effective; however, they are not effective against *T. ishikariensis*. Therefore, in areas where both *Typhula* species occur, the DMI fungicides will not manage *Typhula* blight effectively. Since many greens are a mixture of annual bluegrass and creeping bentgrass, both snow molds, along with all three pathogenic species, may be present. Therefore, it is usually better to use fungicide combinations when trying to control snow mold complexes. A combination that has provided consistent control in trials in northern Michigan has been a one-half rate of a PCNB product and a full rate of chlorothalonil plus a full rate of iprodione.

Fairy Rings

Fairy rings are caused by many fungi in the class Basidomycetes. They cause problems in all turfgrass species. A group of fairy rings known as *superficial fairy rings* have become very problematic on annual bluegrass greens. The *superficial* designation reflects the thin layer of mycelium that typically occurs near the soil surface where this problem is evident. Superficial fairy rings are usually first seen as light yellow or dark green rings, normally ranging in size from a few inches to several feet in diameter. Like most fairy rings, they frequently develop in sandy soil where there is limited microbiological activity or competition.

Superficial fairy rings cause two types of problems on annual bluegrass greens. First, they tend to make the soil hydrophobic, leading to the formation of localized dry spots. Sometimes they will use the thatch as a food source and completely degrade it, leading to sunken areas in the green. This condition is sometimes called *thatch patch*. It occurs because fairy ring-type fungi possess the enzyme ligninase, which is capable of breaking down the lignin-containing organic constituents of thatch.

These fairy rings can usually be managed by drenching in either azoxystrobin or flutolanil. One or the other usually works on most superficial fairy rings, but there have been reports of superficial fairy rings that neither controlled. Some golf course superintendents prefer to treat the symptom rather than the cause and use wetting agents to prevent local dry spots from occurring.

Bacterial Wilt
Pathogen: *Xanthomonas campestris* (Pammel) Dowson.

Bacterial wilt is the only known bacterial disease of annual bluegrass. It can be very devastating when it occurs in the spring, and is a lot more common than generally believed. Fortunately, it usually occurs in late summer or early fall, when very little turf loss occurs; however, it has occurred in the spring and early summer on golf courses in some eastern U.S. locations, where it has caused severe turf loss on infected greens.

SYMPTOMS

The disease is easily recognized by the elongated chlorotic (i.e., etiolated) shoots that extend above the rest of the turfgrass canopy. Despite the fact that this etiolated condition has been observed widely, it is usually not recognized as a symptom of bacterial wilt. In fact, it is rare to be on an annual bluegrass golf course in the late summer or fall and not observe this phenomenon, especially on the fairways. In the United Kingdom and Ireland, where cool and wet conditions persist all year, these symptoms can be seen throughout the growing season. If infected blades are cut and examined under a microscope, bacteria flow coming out of the cut end of the leaves when the coverslip is pressed down can be observed.

OCCURRENCE

Xanthomonas campestris overwinters in infected plants and in the soil. The bacteria apparently build up in the soil during spring and early summer. Following periods of heavy rains in late summer, plants growing in these soils become infected. Bacteria enter the plant through freshly cut xylem vessels during the mowing process or through wounds caused by sand topdressing. Severe outbreaks of bacterial wilt on C-15 (Toronto) creeping bentgrass occurred when golf course superintendents switched from topdressing with soil to the more abrasive sand (Vargas, 1994). Since a sand growth medium has relatively low microbial activity, *X. campestris* populations can build up rapidly in the absence of other potentially competitive organisms. Therefore, topdressing with *X. campestris*–infested sand provides both the bacteria and the wounds through which they can easily enter the plants.

Once inside the xylem vessels within leaves, bacteria can move down to the crowns and roots of the plants. They multiply quickly, plugging up the xylem vessels and reducing the movement of water and nutrients within the plant. This results in a gradual deterioration of the turf during favorable growing conditions, and rapid deterioration during summer when the plants are subjected to heat and drought stresses.

MANAGEMENT: CULTURAL

Since *X. campestris* kills annual bluegrass plants by plugging up the water-conducting xylem vessels, it is advisable to protect annual bluegrass plants infected with bacterial wilt from drought stress through frequent light irrigations.

MANAGEMENT: GENETIC

The only commercially available annual bluegrass cultivar is susceptible to bacterial wilt, especially the first season it is planted.

MANAGEMENT: CHEMICAL

In experimental trials, only oxytetracycline was shown to be effective in controlling bacterial wilt on annual bluegrass. Oxtetracycline is sold as Mycoshield in the agricultural market for the control of certain bacterial diseases of fruits. It is not labeled for use on turfgrass. Several turf specialists have recommended the use of copper products when this disease has become a problem. Not only are the copper products ineffective in controlling this disease, they are also phytotoxic. Injury from copper fungicides can still be evident the second year following application.

Algae

Pathogens: *Phormidium* spp., *Nostoc* spp., and *Oscillatoria* spp.

Algae are minute, threadlike, primitive plants that lack roots, stems, and leaves. Blue-green algae, also known as *cyanobacteria,* are the most commonly occurring in turf.

SYMPTOMS

Algae form a thin, dense, dark green-to-black scum over a soil surface, causing it to become impermeable to air and water exchanges between the soil and the atmosphere. As it dries, a parchmentlike crust forms that may eventually crack and disrupt the surface quality of the turf.

OCCURRENCE

Algae occur primarily on greens, but they can occasionally be found in collars, approaches, and fairways. They are most commonly associated with persistently moist conditions. Although an algae infestation is considered a problem that affects turf in much the same way as do disease-inciting organisms, the algae invade and grow where the turf has thinned or where voids occur from mechanical injury, shade, disease, or insects. The addition of sulfur has been shown to increase algae problems.

MANAGEMENT: CULTURAL

To the extent possible, prevent voids from occurring in turf to minimize exposure of the soil to sunlight. Raise the mowing height for those varieties that are less tolerant of close mowing. It may also be helpful to core-cultivate the "clean-up" pass on greens with ⅜-in. (1-cm) tines monthly during warm weather. Improving the environment around the green by removing trees that shade the green will also help. Good drainage and water management are also necessary, as algae prefer moist conditions. If algae problems persist, check on the levels of sulfur being applied to the turf.

MANAGEMENT: CHEMICAL

The fungicides chlorothalonil and mancozeb have been the most effective chemicals in controlling existing algae problems. To be effective, they should be applied every 2 weeks for as long as the algae problem persists.

INSECTS

White Grubs

White grubs are among the most destructive of all the insect pests feeding on annual bluegrass. White grubs feed on roots and cause damage by destroying the water- and nutrient-absorbing capacity of the plants. White grubs are the larvae of stout-bodied beetles called *scarabs* or *scarabaeids*. The black turfgrass *ataenius, aphodius,* and

Japanese beetles are the most important pests of this group on annual bluegrass. Masked chafers can occasionally cause problems on annual bluegrass turfs, but since they appear to prefer drier turfs, they are more often a problem in roughs than on well-watered greens and fairways where annual bluegrass tends to predominate. The black turfgrass *ataenius* and *aphodius* grubs feed during the warm weather of the summer and can cause considerable loss of annual bluegrass turf. Japanese beetle grubs tend to feed later in the summer when cool nights reduce turf loss. Most of the damage from Japanese beetles occurs from animals and birds tearing up the turf to feed on the grubs. Skunks and crows are particularly destructive of annual bluegrass turfs when searching for grubs.

Black Turfgrass Ataenius (*Ataenius spretulus* Haldeman)

For many years people believed that annual bluegrass died primarily from heat stress during hot summer weather. Niemczyk and Dunbar (1976) and Wegner and Niemczyk (1981) dispelled part of this myth with the discovery of the black turfgrass *ataenius* as a pest of annual bluegrass turfs. Since that time, controlling the black turfgrass *ataenius* has been an important part of maintaining healthy annual bluegrass turfs.

SYMPTOMS

The first indication of the presence of black turfgrass *ataenius* is irregular-shaped patches of wilting annual bluegrass turf (Figure 3.23, see color insert). Cutting into the sod will normally reveal numerous small grubs of the black turfgrass *ataenius* if they are the problem. When black turfgrass *ataenius* grubs are observed, a curative insecticide must be applied immediately. If only water is applied to the wilting turf, the annual bluegrass will continue to wilt and die. These symptoms are first observed from mid-June to mid-July, depending on the location, with the symptoms occurring earlier as one moves toward the equator. In the more southerly regions of the United States, where annual bluegrass is grown, there is normally a second generation of black turfgrass *ataenius* grubs in August. In the more northerly regions of the United States, there is some evidence that there may be one generation of *aphodius* and one generation of black turfgrass *ataenius* rather than two generations of black turfgrass *ataenius*.

Annual Bluegrass Culture

OCCURRENCE

The black turfgrass *ataenius* is found wherever annual bluegrass is grown in North America. The adult beetle actually seems to have a preference for annual bluegrass turfs, although it will also occur in creeping bentgrass, perennial ryegrass, and Kentucky bluegrass turfs. Adults overwinter along the edges of wooded roughs or in woodlots along the perimeter of the golf course under leaves, grass-clipping piles, other debris, or in the upper 2 in. (5 cm) of soil. The black turfgrass beetles begin returning to annual bluegrass fairways and greens following a few warm days in late winter or early spring. The females begin their egg laying about the time when Vanhoutte spirea (*Spiraea vanhouttei*), and horse chestnut (*Aesculus hippocastanum*) come into full bloom, and black locust (*Robinia pseudoacacia*) is showing first bloom.

DESCRIPTION

Adult black turfgrass *ataenius* beetles are small [about $\frac{3}{16}$ in. (4.8 mm) in length and about half as wide] and shiny black in color (Figure 3.24, see color insert). The grubs are approximately ½ in. (12.7 mm) in length, with brown-colored heads (Figure 3.25, see color insert).

MANAGEMENT

Black turfgrass *ataenius* adults and grubs can be controlled with such insecticides as carbaryl, bendiocarb, and chlorpyrifos (Tashiro, 1987; Tashiro et al., 1977). These can be applied prior to the time when Vanhoutte spirea (*Spiraea vanhouttei*) and horse chestnut (*Aesculus hippocastanum*) come into full bloom, and black locust (*Robinia pseudoacacia*) is showing first bloom. Controlling the adult female beetle at this time will prevent egg lay, and no grubs will be present in the turf to cause damage. The insecticide should be washed into the thatch or soil, where the beetles reside, for best results.

A more effective way to manage the beetle is to apply long-residual insecticides, such as imidacloprid in the late spring or halfenozide in early summer. These insecticides should be irrigated into the root zone to be effective. When applied properly, they will control both generations of the black turfgrass *ataenius* grubs or one generation of the black turfgrass *ataenius* and one generation of the *aphodius* grub.

Aphodius Grubs [*Aphodius granarius* (L.) and *Aphodius paradalis* Le Conte]

Like the black turfgrass *ataenius* grubs, *aphodius* grubs can cause serious damage to annual bluegrass turfs (Sears, 1979). These two insects are often found together, and since they look the same to the naked eye, they are often confused for each other.

OCCURRENCE

Research by Smitely and Davis (1999) has shown in Michigan that what used to be considered two generations of the black turfgrass *ataenius* grubs was really one generation of the *aphodius* grubs and one generation of black turfgrass *ataenius* grubs. Based on this research, it appears the damage caused by *aphodius* grubs is more widespread than previously believed and that in cooler regions where annual bluegrass is grown, damage previously attributed to the first generation of black turfgrass *ataenius* grub may actually have been caused by *aphodius* grubs.

Aphodius granaries* has been reported to occur throughout most of the annual bluegrass growing regions of the United States and southern Canada. Most of the damage has been reported on annual bluegrass turfs in the Great Lakes region, including Ontario, Canada, and in the northern Great Plains. *Aphodius pardalis* is reported to cause damage to annual bluegrass turfs on the west coast of the United States (Potter, 1998).

SYMPTOMS

The beetles become active during the first warm days of spring; egg laying follows within 2 to 3 weeks. For all practical purposes the grubs and adults of the black turfgrass *ataenius* and *aphodius* appear similar to all but the trained eye of an entomologist. For a detailed description of how to tell the adults and grubs of these two species apart, see Potter (1998).

In most areas of the country where only one generation of *aphodius* occurs each year, it apparently begins 2 to 3 weeks earlier than the black turfgrass *ataenius*. *Aphodius* adults may be mistaken for black turfgrass *ataenius* adults. Although damage to annual bluegrass turfs occurs from early June through July, it is unclear how much *aphodius* damage has been attributed to the black turfgrass *ataenius*.

MANAGEMENT

Little information is available regarding the control of *aphodius*. However, since the grubs of *aphodius* and the black turfgrass *ataenius* often occur together, or are confused for each other, and since no widespread control failures have been reported for soil insecticides used to control either grub, it can be assumed that soil insecticides that have been reported effective on the black turfgrass *ataenius* are also effective in controlling *aphodius* grubs. See the section "Black Turfgrass *Ataenius*" for more details on using soil insecticides.

Japanese Beetle (*Popillia japonica* Newman)

Japanese beetle grubs can cause problems in annual bluegrass turfs, particularly in the midwestern and eastern United States. Japanese beetle grubs cause typical root-feeding injury. The most severe damage usually appears from late August to early October, after the grubs have attained the third instar. The actual loss of turf due to the Japanese beetle grub will vary from region to region. In cooler regions, by the time the third instar begins feeding, the nighttime temperatures have cooled enough to where very little direct turf loss occurs from the feeding of the grubs. In these regions most of the damage comes from moles, skunks, raccoons, birds (particularly crows), and other animals tearing up the turf to feed on the grubs (Figure 3.26, see color insert). In warmer regions direct loss of turf can occur from Japanese beetle grubs feeding on the annual bluegrass roots (Figure 3.27, see color insert).

OCCURRENCE

The Japanese beetle is native to Japan and was accidentally introduced into the east coast of the United States early in the twentieth century. The eastern U.S. coast provided a favorable climate, turf for developing grubs, many plants for the adults to feed on, and no natural enemies. Japanese beetles thrived on the east coast vegetation and gradually spread across the eastern United States. Japanese beetles are now established in most states east of the Mississippi River. They have also spread northward into Ontario. Rainfall and soil temperature are the factors that will most likely determine the insect's ability to spread beyond its present range. It is unlikely to survive in the semiarid plains or desert regions, except possibly in well-irrigated sites such as golf courses. Isolated occurrences of the beetle have been found in California and Oregon.

DESCRIPTION

The adult beetle is a broadly oval insect, $\frac{5}{16}$ to $\frac{7}{16}$ in. (8 to 11 mm) long and about ¼ in. (6.3 mm) wide (Figure 3.28, see color insert). The head and body are a shiny metallic green. The beetle has coppery brown wings that do not quite cover the tip of the abdomen. For a more detailed description, see Potter (1998).

The larvae are typical grubs, with a white body and a yellowish brown head (Figure 3.29, see color insert). They usually assume a C-shaped position in the soil. Newly hatched grubs are about $\frac{1}{16}$ in. (1.5 mm) long and translucent white; the abdominal area becomes grayish as they feed. As with all white grubs, there are three larval instars. Full-sized, third-instar grubs are about 1 to $1\frac{1}{8}$ in. (25 to 30 mm) long (Potter 1998). They are smaller than masked chafer grubs, but much larger than black turfgrass *ataenius* or *aphodius* grubs.

Japanese beetles have a one-year life cycle in most of the annual bluegrass-growing region. The adult beetles emerge from the soil as adults from mid-June to mid-July in annual bluegrass fairways of the midwestern and eastern United States. They feed for a period of 2 to 4 weeks, depending on the weather. During this time they feed primarily on trees and shrubs on golf courses, with a particular preference for linden and maple trees. Mating and egg laying begin shortly after emergence. Females live 30 to 45 days, during which time they normally lay between 40 and 60 eggs (Potter, 1998). They prefer to lay their eggs in moist soil. Well-irrigated annual bluegrass fairways are ideal for egg laying.

The eggs begin to hatch about 2 weeks after they are laid. The young grubs feed on annual bluegrass roots and organic matter. Most of the grubs will be in the upper 2 in. (5 cm) of soil in well-irrigated annual bluegrass fairways. The grubs molt and become second instars after 2 to 3 weeks, and third instars after 3 to 4 more weeks. They continue to feed into the fall until the first frost. The grubs go deeper into the soil when temperatures cool to about 60°F (15°C). Most grubs overwinter 6 to 8 in. (15.2 to 20.3 cm) below the soil surface. They begin to move back up into the root zone when soil temperatures warm to 50°F (10°C) (Potter, 1998). They will feed on annual bluegrass roots for another 4 to 6 weeks in the spring, then go slightly deeper into the soil to pupate. In regions where annual bluegrass and creeping bentgrass are the predominate fairway species, the life cycle consists mainly of adults and eggs in July, first- and second-instar grubs by mid- to late August, third instars by late August to mid-September, and pupae in mid-May into June.

MANAGEMENT OF ADULTS

On golf courses, Japanese beetles adults cause damage primarily to trees and shrubs. Information concerning control of adults on trees can be found in Potter (1998). However, avoiding the planting of trees that attract beetles, such as lindens and purple plums, may discourage adults flying onto the golf course.

CULTURAL CONTROL OF GRUBS

Since young grubs and eggs need moisture to survive, maintaining annual bluegrass "on the dry side" may help to control grubs during these early stages. However, during the second and third instar stages, when severe loss of roots can occur, it is better to keep the turf moist to prevent severe turf loss.

BIOLOGICAL CONTROL OF GRUBS

From a practical point of view, there are no successful biological controls available at this time. Milky spore treatments have not been very effective; where they have worked, many years were required to reach acceptable levels of control. When nematodes are used for control, timing is critical, since nematodes only remain active for about 3 days. If a system could be developed for continuous applications of nematodes (e.g., through the irrigation system), greater success may be obtained.

On the east coast of the United States, two parasites and two pathogens have been discovered in a natural population of Japanese beetles. These are believed to coincide with natural declines in populations in those areas. Only time will tell if they can be introduced successfully into other areas where Japanese beetles are on the increase.

CHEMICAL CONTROL

As with all grubs, it is easier to kill the younger stages than the mature adults. If curative insecticide treatments are to be applied, the turf should be well irrigated for at least 2 days prior to treatment. This will help ensure that the grubs are feeding near the surface where the insecticide application will be most effective. Although such short-residual insecticides as trichlorfon or carbaryl can be used for curative control, preventive applications of long-residual insecticides such as imidacloprid and halfenozide provide excellent control, since Japanese beetles tend to constitute a reoccurring problem once introduced into an area. Imidacloprid works only preventively and should be applied in late spring or early summer. Halfenozide works best if applied in early summer, but can be applied curatively later in the season.

Annual Bluegrass Weevil [*Listronotus maculicollis* (Dietz) formerly *Hyperodes* sp.]

The other pest that plays an important role in what was previously thought to be heat stress–induced loss of annual bluegrass in summer is the annual bluegrass weevil (ABW). It is especially damaging because it burrows into the crown of the plant, from which new leaves, shoots, and roots arise. With the death of the crown, the entire shoot system is lost, with substantial turf deterioration.

OCCURRENCE

The annual bluegrass weevil has so far been confined to the northeastern United States, including the New England states, New York, New Jersey, and Pennsylvania. It is obvious from watching the spread of the weevil that it is only a matter of time before it spreads westward into other states where annual bluegrass is cultured as a desirable turfgrass species.

The annual bluegrass weevil is mainly a problem on low-cut annual bluegrass on greens and collars (Figure 3.30, see color insert), tees, and fairways (Figure 3.31, see color insert). Very seldom is the weevil a problem in roughs or other turfs mowed above 1.5 in. (3.8 cm). The worst damage usually occurs in the late spring from the first larvae brood. A second generation normally occurs in midsummer, but the damage is usually not as severe.

SYMPTOMS

The adult weevil can cause minor damage to the plant when it feeds at the base of the leaves; however, most of the damage is caused by larvae feeding in the vicinity of the crown (Figure 3.32, see color insert). With sufficient feeding in this area, shoots may become easily separated from the roots.

The adult ABW beetles are $\frac{1}{8}$ to $\frac{5}{32}$ inch (3.2 to 4.0 mm) in length and charcoal gray in color (Figure 3.33, see color insert). When the first adults emerge, they are light brown; as they age, they eventually develop a shiny black appearance. ABW beetles somewhat resemble billbugs; however, they have a short, broad snout, whereas billbugs have a long snout. The legless larvae are creamy white in color, C-shaped, with a brown head. The larvae reach a length of about $\frac{3}{16}$ in. (4.8 mm) when fully developed (Potter, 1998).

MANAGEMENT

The ABW is best managed in areas of known occurrence with long residual insecticides such as imidacloprid and halfenozide. These insecticides should be applied when the adults are actively feeding in the spring. Short-residual insecticides may also be used, but the timing is more critical since they will have little effect once the eggs have been laid in the crown. A biological timing indicator for insecticide application is to apply the insecticide between the time the forsythia is blooming and dogwood is in full bloom (Potter, 1998). Traps may also be used to monitor spring migration of the ABW adults. For more information on chemical control, see Table 3.4.

Black Cutworm [*Agrostis ipsilon* (Hufnagel)]

Black cutworms cause damage on annual bluegrass greens by chewing the grass shoots down to the ground. Black cutworms tend to live in coring holes. They emerge at night and feed on the turfgrass around the coring hole, making the hole more visible. In addition to "scalping" the turf, the damage also makes for a very uneven putting surface, which interferes with ball roll.

OCCURRENCE

Black cutworm occurs through the United States, Canada, Europe, Asia, Africa, and everywhere else annual bluegrass is cultivated. There can be up to six generations per season in the southern United States and as few as two generations in parts of the northern United States and Canada. The black cutworm does not overwinter in the colder regions of the United States; reinfestation occurs from adults

TABLE 3.4

Guide to Controlling Annual Bluegrass Insects

Insecticide	Insect						
	Annual Bluegrass Weevils	Ants	Aphodius Grubs	Black Turfgrass *ataenius*	Cutworms	Japanese Beetles	Sod Webworms
Azadirachtin					×		×
Bacillus thuringiensis					×		×
Bendiocarb		×	×	×		×	
Bifenthrin		×			×		×
Carbaryl		×	×	×	×	×	×
Chlorpyrifos	×	×			×		×
Cyfluthrin	×	×			×		×
Deltamethrin		×					
Ethoprop			×	×	×	×	×
Halfenozide			×	×		×	
Imidacloprid	×		×	×		×	
Isofenphos					×		×
Lambda-cyhalothrin	×	×			×		×
Permethrin		×			×		×
Soap					×		×
Spinosad					×		×
Trichlorfon	×		×	×	×	×	×

being carried by prevailing winds from the southwest. Adult moths can be carried several hundred miles. Black cutworms feed on annual bluegrass greens, tees, and fairways; however, noticeable damage is evident only on greens unless infestations on tees and fairways are exceptionally heavy.

SYMPTOMS

The black cutworm larvae chew the turfgrass shoots down to the soil in the areas surrounding a coring hole (Figure 3.34, see color insert). Examination of the hole may reveal green fecal pellets left by the larvae. In coring holes with newly developed symptoms the black cutworms themselves can usually be found. The larvae are approximately 1 to 2 in. (2.5 to 5.0 cm) in length, smooth in appearance, gray to black in color, with a pale stripe down the middle of their backs (Figure 3.35, see color insert). When disturbed, the black cutworm larvae tend to curl into a ball.

MANAGEMENT: BIOLOGICAL

Entomopathogentic nematodes such as *Steinernema carpocapsae* have been somewhat effective in providing biological control of black cutworm populations. A constant problem with using biologicals is understanding how they work. First, the nematodes should be active; second, they should be applied as close to nightfall as possible, since ultraviolet light from the sun can kill them. They should be watered in the evening following application, although they can often survive in the dew or guttation water the next morning. If they dry out in the daylight, they will typically die. The nematode will remain active for about 3 days. If cutworm activity continues beyond 3 days, an additional application of the nematode will be necessary.

Azadirachtin, or Neem, is a natural pesticide that has been derived from the neem tree. Is has low mammalian and wildlife toxicity. It works by disrupting the black cutworm's molting process. It is most effective against young molting larvae. To be effective it should be applied as close to dark as possible and not watered in.

MANAGEMENT: CHEMICAL

Black cutworms are normally controlled using curative insecticide applications when damage is first noticed. Many insecticides are effective in controlling cutworms; they are listed in Table 3.4.

CHAPTER 4
Annual Bluegrass Control

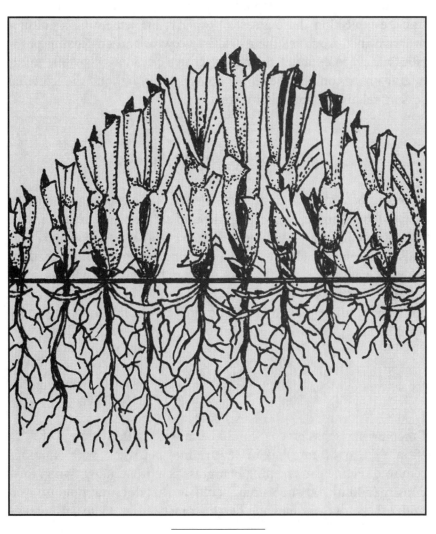

A NNUAL BLUEGRASS populations are best controlled by maximizing the resistance of the particular turfgrass species or cultivar employed for greens, tees, or fairways to its invasion and subsequent growth. This requires careful adherence to the fundamentals of turfgrass management: selecting turfgrass species and cultivars that are well adapted to prevailing environmental conditions, establishing these grasses properly, implementing a cultural program that promotes their healthy growth, and employing pesticides wisely to enhance their competitive advantages—while minimizing their competitive disadvantages—throughout the growing season, relative to annual bluegrass.

CREEPING BENTGRASS

Creeping bentgrass (*Agrostis stolonifera* L.) is a cool-season species adapted to subarctic, temperate, and cool-subtropical climatic zones. It does best in sunny locations with moist, fertile, acid to slightly acid soils. As it tolerates close mowing, creeping bentgrass can be used for greens as well as tees and fairways. Although its growth habit is stoloniferous, it varies widely in shoot growth orientation, with some cultivars tending toward prostrate growth while others are more upright.

Mowing

Greens

Creeping bentgrass greens should be mowed within a range of $\frac{1}{10}$ to $\frac{3}{16}$ in. (2.5 to 4.8 mm) six or seven times per week, with clippings removed. Penncross creeping bentgrass is a prostrate-growing, low-density (600 to 900 shoots/dm^2) cultivar that does not hold up well under the very close mowing heights practiced on many golf greens today. Medium-density (1200 to 1600 shoots/dm^2), upright-growing cultivars, including Pennlinks, Providence, Putter, and L-93, are marginal when mowed at $\frac{1}{8}$ in. (3.18 mm) or less and are probably more suited to $\frac{5}{32}$ in. (4.00 mm) or above for best competition with annual bluegrass. The problem with mowing greens at higher heights is that the speed requirements of today's greens cannot be met without employing supplemental practices. Such practices as applying plant growth regulators and rolling could be used as alternatives to closer mowing; otherwise, the shoot densities of these cultivars may decline and allow annual bluegrass invasion.

The newer Penn A- and G-series are high-density (2200 to 2800 shoots/dm^2) upright-growing creeping bentgrasses that tolerate very close mowing and summer heat-stress levels typical of vast regions within the subtropical climatic zone. Because of the large number of tillers produced at low mowing heights, this group of cultivars is able to sustain high shoot densities when mowed at $\frac{1}{8}$ in. (3.18 mm) or below. Although they are more competitive with annual bluegrass at these mowing heights, some hand weeding is still needed to keep these greens completely free of annual bluegrass.

Greens that are mowed routinely with walk-behind greens mowers, which impose less stress than riding triplex mowers, are of generally higher quality; however, the cleanup lap can still be stressed due to the additional traffic associated with daily mowing.

Fairways

Creeping bentgrass fairways should be mowed within a range of $\frac{3}{8}$ to $\frac{5}{8}$ in. (9.5 to 16 mm) three to five times per week, preferably with clippings removed. Tremendous increases in the creeping bentgrass population of fairways have been observed where lightweight mowers were used in place of gang mowers or larger attached units. The soil compaction caused by the heaver equipment favors annual bluegrass over creeping bentgrass. Most fairways are currently mowed with lightweight five-unit mowers. A few golf courses mow their fairways with triplex greens mowers. Some courses have resorted to mowing approaches with walking greens mowers. The five-unit fairway mowers have increased the creeping bentgrass content of the fairways compared with the larger fairway mowers; triplex mowers have increased the creeping bentgrass content of the fairways even more, and mowing approaches with walking greens mowers has provided further increases. Regardless of the species, the quality of the fairway turf improves incrementally as the mowers change from tractor-drawn gang units to fiveplex, then to triplex, and finally to walking greens mowers.

Collecting clippings has also increased the creeping bentgrass content of fairways compared with returning clippings (Gaussoin, 1988). Although the scientific basis for this effect is not fully understood, clipping removal would reduce canopy temperature, inoculum from infected leaves, nutrients from clipping decomposition, and the accumulation of annual bluegrass seed available for subsequent germination. Also, where clipping production is especially heavy due to weather-related interruptions in the mowing schedule, light exclusion and associated loss of turf are avoided by removing clippings.

Fertilization

Greens

Since creeping bentgrass has a lower nitrogen requirement than that required for optimum growth and competitive ability of annual bluegrass, a relatively lean nitrogen fertility program should be followed to favor the creeping bentgrass. This usually entails "spoon feeding" soluble nitrogen at rates of $\frac{1}{10}$ to $\frac{1}{8}$ lb N per 1000 ft^2 (49 to 61 g N per 100 m^2) every 2 weeks during the growing season. Nitrogen fertilization should be sufficient to sustain a shoot growth rate yielding 0.7 to 1.0 basket of clippings per day from a green measuring approximately 6000 ft^2 (558 m^2) (Beard, 2002). Although higher N rates applied when annual bluegrass seed heads are beginning to form might be effective in exploiting a competitive advantage in favor of creeping bentgrass, the reduced putting speeds associated with stimulated shoot growth would, in most cases, eliminate this as a feasible option.

Other primary—as well as secondary and tertiary—nutrients should be provided as part of a balanced fertility program, as suggested by soil and plant-tissue test results. Tissue concentrations of these nutrients in excess of those considered optimum for creeping bentgrass should be avoided, as they may be phytotoxic to creeping bentgrass or favor the growth and competitive ability of annual bluegrass. Among the tertiary nutrients, iron is the one most likely to be deficient, especially on very sandy or alkaline soils. Incorporating iron with fungicide sprays can correct deficiencies and produce darker green foliage without promoting the faster shoot growth associated with nitrogen applications. There is some evidence suggesting that iron applications enhance the growth of creeping bentgrass more than annual blugrass, thus providing a competitive advantage for creeping bentgrass in mixed communities with annual bluegrass (Xu and Mancino, 2001).

Soil reaction should be managed to sustain the pH within a range of 5.5 to 6.5 for optimum growth of creeping bentgrass, with lime used to raise the pH to the optimum range where necessary. Lowering the pH value of alkaline soils with high cation-exchange capacities through the use of sulfur or ammonium sulfate can be quite difficult, especially where calcareous sands were used for construction or topdressing, and excess sulfur can lead to black layer formation.

Fairways

As in greens, light applications of soluble nitrogen ($\frac{1}{8}$ to $\frac{1}{4}$ lb per 1000 ft^2; 61 to 122 g per 100 m^2) should be made every 2 weeks to sustain healthy growth of creeping bentgrass and avoid excessive stimulation of annual bluegrass. The exception to this is when annual bluegrass seed heads are forming; higher soluble nitrogen rates (0.5 lb per 1000 ft^2, 0.54 kg per 100 m^2) applied at this time can exploit the competitive advantage of creeping bentgrass by stimulating its growth when annual bluegrass is unable to respond vegetatively.

Other primary—as well as secondary and tertiary—nutrients should be provided as part of a balanced fertility program, as suggested by soil and plant-tissue test results. Excessive use of phosphorus should be avoided, as this may favor annual bluegrass. Potassium applications in excess of recommendations based on soil tests are sometimes advocated because of the special importance that potassium has in enhancing turfgrass tolerance to environmental stress—including wear, heat, and drought stresses—during the summer months. A rule of thumb is to apply potassium routinely at 75 to 100 percent of the nitrogen application rate (Beard, 2002), and many superintendents are now using potassium rates at 100 to 200 percent of the nitrogen rate. In summer, potassium sulfate (K_2SO_4) is preferable to potassium chloride (KCl), due to its substantially lower salt index and therefore reduced foliar burn potential. An additional benefit from the use of the sulfate carrier is the added contribution of sulfur to the fertilization program.

Among the tertiary nutrients, iron is the one most likely to be deficient during the midsummer stress period. Research results at Ohio State University suggest that monthly applications of iron (0.55 oz Fe per 1000 ft^2; 17 g per 100 m^2), or a combination of iron and magnesium at these same rates, provided creeping bentgrass with a competitive advantage over annual bluegrass under fairway management (Bell et al., 1997).

Soil reaction should be managed to sustain the pH within the range 5.5 to 6.5 for optimum growth of creeping bentgrass, with sulfur or ammonium sulfate used to lower the pH and lime used to raise it as necessary.

Irrigation

Greens

Although irrigation is certainly important for satisfying the moisture requirements of a creeping bentgrass turf, providing adequate internal and surface drainage is an equally important component of a water-management program. Poor drainage over extended periods means that soil aeration will be inadequate to sustain healthy bentgrass root growth. As a consequence, annual bluegrass, which is more tolerant of persistently wet soils, will have a competitive advantage. Therefore, two interrelated elements must exist to ensure satisfactory water management: a properly constructed irrigation system for uniformly distributing water at rates equal to or below the infiltration capacity of the turf, and a properly constructed green that can accommodate rapid percolation of water through the profile, along with slightly sloping topography to provide surface drainage during major rainfall events. Then, an irrigation program should be established to sustain sufficient growth for playable shoot density.

Fairways

As with greens, an irrigation program should be established to sustain sufficient growth while ensuring that fairway drainage is adequate to avoid oxygen deficiencies in the root zone that might otherwise favor annual bluegrass. Irrigation systems that fail to distribute water uniformly over the fairway often overwater some areas while underwatering others; as a consequence, the growth and competitive capacity of creeping bentgrass may be affected adversely and annual bluegrass favored. With a combination of overwatering and shade, annual bluegrass is favored even more.

Topdressing

Greens

Creeping bentgrass is a thatch-forming species. Excessive thatch must be controlled if healthy turf is to be maintained. Where a substantial thatch layer exists, turfgrass crowns are elevated above the soil surface and the thatch becomes the primary medium supporting turfgrass growth. As thatch is highly porous and does not retain moisture well, turfgrasses growing in thatch are subjected to wide fluctuations in plant-available moisture. Under these conditions, especially during prolonged dry periods in summer, thatchy turfs are highly susceptible to deterioration from heat and drought stresses. Also, thatch can become hydrophobic when allowed to dry completely; as a consequence, it tends to repel water and remain dry, despite frequent or intensive irrigations.

In addition to moisture, thatch does not retain nutrients well. As soluble nutrients tend to leach readily from the thatch, turfgrasses with their roots confined largely to the thatch layer may exhibit nutrient deficiencies, despite the nutrient content of the underlying soil.

Thatchy creeping bentgrass turfs are highly susceptible to disease. As many disease-inciting organisms can survive on organic residues until conditions favor disease development, thatch provides an ideal environment for the saprophytic growth of these organisms.

Thatch can also result in puffiness and footprinting on greens, which will adversely affect putting and predispose the green to scalping from mowing. Scalping produces voids in the turf that are often filled by annual bluegrass. In addition to the normally occurring thatch, creeping bentgrass also produces a "transitory" thatch during warm summer weather, resulting in a convoluted, "puffy" surface that dramatically increases the turf's susceptibility to scalping from mowing. With scalping in late summer, entry windows are created for annual bluegrass invasion as soon as temperatures favor germination.

The most effective means of managing thatch is through top-dressing. Greens consisting of Penncross and the medium-density upright-growing creeping bentgrasses should be topdressed every 2 to 3 weeks, requiring 0.05 to 0.1 yd^3 per 1000 ft^2 (0.035 to 0.07 m^3 per 1000 m^2) (Beard, 2002). This varies depending on season and turfgrass growth rate; more frequent topdressings are required during spring and fall when creeping bentgrass is growing more vig-orously, and less frequent applications can be made during the summer when growth may be slower. The high-density upright-growing creeping bentgrasses (Penn A- and G-series) produce large amounts of thatch and require light topdressing on almost a weekly basis to prevent thatch buildup and associated scalping and layering problems. Because of the high shoot density of these cultivars, some vertical mowing may be required to facilitate incorporation of the topdressing soil into the turf.

Through topdressing, soil (more typically, sand or loamy sand) is used to modify the thatch in much the same way that organic matter can be used to modify a soil to improve its properties as a growth medium. Soil particles fill in some of the larger pores perme-ating the thatch medium, resulting in a thatchlike derivative (some-times referred to as *mat*) with vastly different properties. Moisture and nutrient retention are improved; a firmer medium, less vulnera-ble to footprinting, scalping, and disease, is created; and the bio-decomposition rate of the organic materials comprising the original thatch is accelerated. With an overall improvement in the health of the creeping bentgrass population, its resistance to annual bluegrass invasion is increased correspondingly.

It is important to ensure that the soil used for topdressing is either consistent with the underlying soil, or is coarser-textured (e.g., where a sandy mix is used for topdressing a pushup green composed of a finer-textured medium), to avoid troublesome textural layers in the soil profile. Where a finer-textured medium is positioned above a coarser-textured one, water moving through the finer-textured medium will stop when it reaches the interface of the two media and form a perched water table. Conversely, where a coarser-textured medium is positioned above a finer-textured one, water moving through the coarser-textured medium will move into and through the finer-textured one at a slower rate, perhaps resulting in a temporary water table above the interface of the two media. Therefore, to ensure proper internal drainage, topdressing materials should be consistent over time to ensure textural uniformity within the soil profile.

Fairways

Fairways are not typically topdressed due to the enormous cost associated with this practice on extensive sites. They are normally core-cultivated instead, with the cores reincorporated for thatch management. However, topdressing fairways with sand is becoming a common practice on golf courses in regions of the world with high annual rainfall, especially where the underlying soil is poorly drained.

Cultivation

Greens

To favor creeping bentgrass over annual bluegrass, core cultivation should be timed to take place during the spring seed-production window for annual bluegrass. At this time, photoassimilates are directed at supporting reproductive growth and development (through which seed heads are produced), which occurs at the expense of vegetative growth and development. Since coring stimulates vegetative growth, the strictly vegetatively growing creeping bentgrass population can favorably respond to it at this time, whereas the reproductively growing annual bluegrass cannot. With the enhanced shoot and root growth from spring coring, the creeping bentgrass population is better situated to withstand the summer-stress period.

Most annual bluegrass seed germination takes place within a temperature range of 60 to 70°F (16 to 21°C) at the 1-in. (2.5-cm) soil depth. Depending on geographic location, this occurs in mid- to late spring and again in late summer to early fall. Core cultivations occurring within this temperature window bring up soil that contains annual bluegrass seed, exposing it to sunlight and allowing it to germinate and invade a creeping bentgrass turf. Conversely, core cultivations performed outside this window are less likely to favor annual bluegrass seed germination, and thus the competitive advantage that annual bluegrass might otherwise realize has been lost.

Many golf course superintendents core cultivate in the fall to relieve soil compaction and stimulate plant growth. If coring were not performed at this time, however, alternate freezing-and-thawing cycles during the winter would provide at least some relief of compaction, with new root initiation taking place the following spring. If the goal is to have greens free of annual bluegrass, coring greens during the annual bluegrass fall germination window would be counterproductive. Many golf courses have greatly reduced annual bluegrass invasion of creeping bentgrass greens simply by eliminating fall coring or by replacing it with coring in late summer, when annual bluegrass germination is less likely.

Coring intensity varies with the diameter and length of the tines used for cultivation. Tine diameter ranges from ¼ to ⅝ in. (6.4 to 15.9 mm) for conventional core cultivators, and up to 1.5 in. (38 mm) for deep-coring (e.g., Verti-Drain) units. Conventional core cultivators penetrate to a maximum depth of 3 to 4 in. (75 to 100 mm), while deep-coring units may penetrate to a depth of 10 to 16 in. (250 to 400 mm). Cultivation tines include both hollow and solid versions. Hollow-tine cultivators extract soil cores from the turf, causing some compression of the soil at the maximum depth of penetration and along the walls of the holes. With repeated use, a *cultivation pan* may develop several inches below the soil surface. Solid tines potentially cause even more soil compression. However, if used when the soil is dry, the uplifting of the soil mass that takes place as the tines are extracted may cause some fracturing and thus alleviate soil compaction. Good topdressing programs can reduce the adverse effects of cultivation pans by incrementally raising the soil surface, thereby changing the depth that the tines reach. Because of the disruption of the turf's surface caused by core cultivation, this operation is best done during cool weather when heat and drought stress are at a minimum and conditions are favorable for rapid recovery. If warm-weather coring is necessary, smaller tines should be used to minimize surface disruptions and the increased potential for bentgrass desiccation.

Following hollow-tine core cultivation the soil cores may be removed and the holes filled with topdressing soil, or the cores may be reincorporated into the turf through vertical mowing and subsequent matting operations. On push-up greens, reincorporation of soil cores may be acceptable, provided that the core soil is the same as that used for topdressing; otherwise, troublesome layers may be created where topdressing soil and native soil are superimposed one on top of the other. On sand-based greens, the cores are often removed to replace "dirty" sand with "clean" sand from topdressing. In this way, satisfactory infiltration rates can be maintained and excessive accumulations of organic residues in the top several inches of sand controlled.

An alternative to summertime coring with tine cultivators is the use of water-injection cultivators (e.g., Toro's HydroJect) that inject 10-millisecond pulses of highly pressurized water into the turf. The result is small channels through which improvements in aeration porosity and infiltration may be realized.

Finally, drill cultivators have been developed that employ drills in place of tines to probe deeply into the turf, extract and deposit large quantities of soil onto the surface, and backfill the holes with sand. These can be used to create sand columns for providing bypass drainage through an impermeable or slowly permeable medium to reach a more permeable medium below.

Fairways

Coring in the spring with the cores matted back in is important for alleviating soil compaction and managing thatch on creeping bentgrass fairways. The soil generated from coring operations can substitute for topdressing soil. With its reincorporation into the turf, the edaphic properties of the thatch are ameliorated and biodecomposition of the organic residues comprising the thatch is accelerated.

The timing of the core cultivations should coincide with the initiation of annual bluegrass seed head production to stimulate the vegetative growth of the creeping bentgrass population at a time when annual bluegrass is at a competitive disadvantage.

Rolling

Rolling is done for a variety of purposes, including smoothing the surface of a green and improving putting speed. Where surface disruptions have been caused by cultivation practices, rolling can be helpful in reestablishing a smooth surface and avoiding injury from subsequent mowing operations. Otherwise, infestation ports may be created through which annual bluegrass may gain entry by germinating from seed and forming new colonies within the turfgrass community. Care must be taken to ensure that rolling operations do not cause such severe soil compaction that the growth of creeping bentgrass is adversely affected and, as a consequence, annual bluegrass derives a competitive advantage.

Chemical Control of Annual Bluegrass

Greens

The chemicals that might be used to control annual bluegrass infestations in creeping bentgrass turfs include herbicides and plant-growth regulators (PGRs). On greens, however, the potential for phytotoxicity from herbicides is high and their use is far more limited than for fairways and other turfs. Postemergence herbicides have been used at various times, often with unacceptable phytotoxicity. A new herbicide, bispyribac, commercially available as Velocity, shows some promise for selectively controlling annual bluegrass in mixed stands with creeping bentgrass. Extreme care must be exercised to avoid unacceptable phytotoxicity to the bentgrass. Where large patches of annual bluegrass exist, their sudden loss from herbicide treatment would leave voids requiring immediate overseeding and sufficient time for successful establishment of new bentgrass populations. With only small voids, recovery would depend on sufficient vegetative growth of adjacent bentgrass plants to fill the voids completely.

To the extent that they are used, preemergence herbicides—typically, bensulide (Bensumec, Pre-San)—are applied in late summer to control annual bluegrass emerging from fall seed germination; however, control is often unsatisfactory in greens where annual bluegrass is a well-established component of the turfgrass community (Dernoeden, 2000). Presumably, this reflects the predominance of perennial biotypes of annual bluegrass that depend less on seed germination as a vehicle for sustaining their presence in greens. Also, the residual activity of preemergence herbicides can conflict with overseeding practices, especially where winter injury occurs, leaving large areas of dead turf in the spring. If winter injury does not occur, herbicide residues may delay or retard bentgrass rooting, especially during cool wet weather and on poorly drained sites. Where preemergence herbicides are also applied in the spring, there is an additional risk of phytotoxicity during hot summer weather. Because of these concerns, on new creeping bentgrass greens where the annual bluegrass population is small, mechanical removal of individual plants or small clumps of annual bluegrass with a knife, or spot treatment with glufosinate ammonium (Finale) applied with a blotter pen, is often the preferred way of controlling annual bluegrass.

With respect to PGRs, paclobutrazol (Trimmit, Turf Enhancer) can be applied two or three times in the spring, but most important, just after annual bluegrass seed shatter in spring to keep it in a "weakened condition" while stimulating the stolon growth of creeping bentgrass to enhance its competitive advantage, and two or three times in late summer and early fall to suppress the growth of newly germinated annual bluegrass plants (Watschke, personal communication, 2002). An application of nitrogen at the rate of 0.3 lb N per 1000 ft^2 (147 g per 100 m^2) is also recommended at this time to ensure that sufficiently aggressive stolon growth of the bentgrass takes place. By midfall, nitrogen fertility should be kept at a minimum to avoid stimulating the growth of annual bluegrass when bentgrass growth slows in response to cool temperatures, short daylengths, and frost.

Some golf course superintendents have observed that the efficacy of paclobutrazol for suppressing annual bluegrass selectively in creeping bentgrass greens diminishes over time. This may reflect the selective survival of greens-type stoloniferous perennial biotypes of annual bluegrass that respond to paclobutrazol in much the same way as creeping bentgrass; while vertical shoot growth is suppressed, lateral stolon growth is sufficiently stimulated to enable *this* component of the annual bluegrass population to persist and compete with creeping bentgrass. Biostimulants containing gibberellic acid should not be used where paclobutrazol has been applied, as they will counteract the effects of this gibberellic acid biosynthesis-inhibiting PGR.

Fairways

As with greens, the chemicals that might be used to control annual bluegrass infestations in creeping bentgrass fairways include herbicides and PGRs; however, the number of alternatives for fairways is greater. With respect to preemergence herbicides, two applications are required to provide season-long control of annual bluegrass; these usually include a full-rate application in mid- to late August and a half-rate application in late April or early May. Dithiopyr (Dimension) and several dinitroaniline herbicides, including benefin and trifluralin (Team), pendimethalin (Pre-M, Pendulum), and prodiamine (Barricade), are used for controlling annual bluegrass as well as summer annual grasses. Oxadiazon (Ronstar) can also be used; while some leaf tip burn may be evident in summer following spring applications of this material, it does not cause the root growth inhibition characteristic of many other preemergence herbicides (Branham, personal communication, 2001). With season-long control from preemergence herbicides, however, opportunities to introduce creeping bentgrass from seed are precluded. Also, efficacy from preemergence herbicides is limited to annual bluegrass emerging from seed germination. Established populations are largely unaffected, except perhaps for some enhanced reduction of turf quality during summer stress periods. Any disruption of the turf from divots or other causes also breaks the chemical barrier, allowing annual bluegrass seed to germinate despite the presence of preemergence herbicide residues nearby.

Ethofumesate (Progress) can be used for achieving partial control of established populations of annual bluegrass—principally the annual biotypes—in creeping bentgrass fairways. Because creeping bentgrass is not as tolerant of this herbicide as perennial ryegrass, lower rates (i.e., not more than 0.75 lb a.i. per acre or 0.84 kg a.i. per ha) must be used; as a consequence, its efficacy is less than where higher rates can be used. Two to three applications, 21 days apart, are typically made in the fall. This reflects the role that cold temperatures play in the control achieved from ethofumesate; where mild temperatures follow ethofumesate applications, little control may be evident, while very good control has often resulted where severe winter temperatures have occurred.

Inconsistent results from ethofumesate applications suggest that other factors may influence its activity. One possibility is resistance, sometimes acquired by plant populations from prolonged use of herbicides.

Creeping bentgrass is often discolored by applications of ethofumesate. This is most evident in poorly rooted, shaded, waterlogged, heavily trafficked, or diseased turfs. Discoloration can be reduced by undertaking measures to correct these problems and by co-applying chelated iron or light rates of soluble nitrogen with ethofumesate. Different creeping bentgrass cultivars vary in their sensitivity. Pennlinks and Penneagle are less tolerant than Penncross. Other bentgrass species (e.g., colonial, velvet) are intolerant and should not be treated with this herbicide.

Since treated turfs should not be overseeded for at least 2 weeks following the last ethofumesate application, fall applications may require delaying seeding until the following spring. Where large expanses of annual bluegrass occur, effective control with ethofumesate would have a disastrous effect on turf quality, requiring extensive overseeding to reestablish turfgrass cover. Ethofumesate is best used where annual bluegrass populations are small and recovery from the growth of adjacent creeping bentgrass populations can be achieved fairly rapidly. To the extent that extensive spring overseeding might be necessary, one should consider the use of clear plastic covers to accelerate turfgrass germination and seedling development.

As discussed under greens, bispyribac could be used for selectively controlling annual bluegrass in mixed stands with creeping bentgrass; however, because of limited experience with this herbicide, it should be used experimentally on small areas before broadening its use to encompass an entire golf course. Because Kentucky bluegrass is more sensitive to this herbicide than creeping bentgrass, its selectivity for controlling annual bluegrass in turfs containing Kentucky bluegrass is reduced substantially.

With respect to PGRs, certain gibberellic acid biosynthesis inhibitors have shown the greatest utility for selectively suppressing the growth of annual bluegrass in mixed stands with creeping bentgrass. The class B PGR paclobutrazol (Trimmet, Turf Enhancer) inhibits cell elongation by interfering with gibberellic acid biosynthesis; as a consequence, vertical shoot growth of turfgrasses, and thus their mowing requirements, are reduced. Where the annual bluegrass population is made up primarily of annual biotypes, paclobutrazol can suppress its growth while simultaneously stimulating lateral shoot (i.e., stolon) growth of adjacent creeping bentgrass plants. Paclobutrazol can be applied two or three times in spring, but it is most important that it be done just after annual bluegrass seed shatter (as with greens), and two or three times in late summer and early fall to suppress the growth of newly germinated annual bluegrass plants. As turfgrass response can vary with soil type, climatic conditions, moisture levels, application timing, and other factors, careful experimentation should be done to establish how this material can best be used as part of an annual bluegrass control program (Diesburg and Christians, 1989).

Where it is desirable to convert a predominantly annual bluegrass fairway to creeping bentgrass through a complete renovation or reestablishment procedure, dazomet (Basamid Granular) may be used to kill the annual bluegrass seed reservoir in the soil. To ensure efficacy, treated sites must be sealed to prevent the methyl isocyanate (MITC) gas released from the formulation from escaping into the atmosphere. This can be accomplished by covering the soil with a tarp for 5 to 7 days following application, or by employing irrigation to seal the surface for 4 to 5 days following application. Seeding can take place after the MITC gas has dissipated.

Finally, glyphosate- and glufosinate-tolerant creeping bentgrasses are under development. When they are commercially available, they will allow the selective removal of annual bluegrass from newly established or overseeded fairways. Although this offers a powerful new tool for controlling annual bluegrass, one cannot help but wonder how soon glyphosate- and glufosinate-tolerant annual bluegrasses will evolve.

Biological Control of Annual Bluegrass

Biological control of annual bluegrass can be attempted by maximizing disease pressure that is specific to annual bluegrass in mixed stands with creeping bentgrass (Dernoeden, 2000). When diseases occur to which annual bluegrass is selectively susceptible, such as summer patch (*Magnaporthe poae*) and annual bluegrass-specific forms of anthracnose (*Colletotrichum graminicola*) and bacterial wilt (*Xanthomonas campestris*), fungicides may be withheld to enhance the competitive advantage of creeping bentgrass during the summer; this assumes that the annual bluegrass population is small, and its loss will not result in an unacceptable decline in the appearance and playability of the turf. Light rates of soluble nitrogen (0.1 to 0.15 lb per 1000 ft^2; 49 to 74 g per 100 m^2) should be applied every week or two to stimulate the growth of creeping bentgrass and ensure that it can fully exploit its competitive advantage.

A second possible approach to biological control of annual bluegrass is through the use of XPoM bioherbicide (Eco Soil Systems), a commercial formulation of the annual bluegrass-specific form of *X. campestris*, called *Xanthomonas campestris* pv. *poanna*. Successive applications can cause infections that weaken plants and make them more susceptible to mortality from cold stress in winter and heat and drought stresses during summer (Mitra and Vrabel, 2000). Initial symptoms are observed as etiolation of flowering culms, followed by chlorosis and epinasty of affected plants. Both annual and perennial biotypes of annual bluegrass are susceptible. Factors that appear to increase infection and mortality from XPoM are moderate temperatures (64 to 88°F, 24 to 31°C) at the time of application, mowing the turf immediately after application to provide openings for easy movement of the bacterium into the tissue, low irrigation levels to induce moisture stress, and the application of paclobutrazol PGR or ethofumisate to weaken the annual bluegrass. From numerous studies conducted throughout North America and in Europe, results from the use of this material have varied widely, with many researchers finding no efficacy on established stands of annual bluegrass.

Controlling Other Weeds

Greens

On greens, crabgrass and goosegrass may be controlled primarily by mechanical means (i.e., knifing or plugging out). Clovers, mouse-ear chickweed, and other broadleaf weeds can be controlled with postemergence applications of mecoprop as needed and in accordance with label directions. Because of the potential for phytotoxicity, most other phenoxycarboxylic acid and related herbicides should not be used on greens.

Fairways

In addition to their role in controlling annual bluegrass during periods of seed germination, preemergence herbicides can be used for preventing the emergence of summer annual grasses, including crabgrass and goosegrass, and an array of broadleaf weeds. These herbicides include dithiopyr (Dimension), several dinitroaniline herbicides, including benefin and trifluralin (Team), pendimethalin (Pre-M, Pendulum), and prodiamine (Barricade), and oxadiazon (Ronstar). As discussed earlier, some leaf tip burn may be evident in summer following spring applications of oxadiazon, but this material does not cause the root growth inhibition characteristic of other preemergence herbicides (Branham, personal communication, 2001).

Postemergence control of newly germinated stands of crabgrass in creeping bentgrass fairways can be obtained from applications of fenoxyprop p-ethyl (Acclaim Extra); however, its efficacy declines as crabgrass plants mature and produce more tillers. Efficacy is also reduced under droughty conditions or if fenoxyprop p-ethyl is mixed with 2,4-D and related phenoxycarboxylic acid herbicides. Well-established crabgrass (i.e., more than four tillers) is more easily controlled with postemergence applications of quinclorac (Drive). Dithiopyr is unique among the preemergence herbicides in that it also provides some early postemergence activity. Where dithiopyr is applied to untillered crabgrass especially or to crabgrass with no more than two tillers, satisfactory control can be achieved. A possible alternative to conventional preemergence herbicides for crabgrass control is corn gluten meal (CGM), a by-product of corn wet milling containing a series of dipeptides that inhibit mitosis in root tips. Because of the very high application rates required for effective weed control, however, the amount of nitrogen also applied through this material is likely to be excessive.

Postemergence control of young populations of goosegrass germinating throughout the summer can be obtained from applications of fenoxyprop p-ethyl at light rates every 2 weeks. These applications could be made in combination with fungicides where disease control is needed.

Clover, chickweed, and other broadleaf weeds can be controlled with postemergence applications of selected phenoxycarboxylic acid (mecoprop, dichloroprop), pyridinecarboxylic acid (triclopyr, clopyralid), quinolinecarboxylic acid (quinclorac), benzoic acid (dicamba), and aryltriazolinone (carfentrazone) herbicides applied in combinations or, in some cases, individually.

Disease Control

Creeping bentgrass greens are highly susceptible to several important diseases, including brown patch (*Rhizoctonia solani*), dollar spot (*Rutstroemia floccosum*), leaf spot (*Bipolaris sorokiniana*), *Pythium* blight (*Pythium* spp.), *Typhula* blight (*Typhula incarnata, T. ishikarienis*), *Microdocium* patch (*Microdocium nivale*), and take-all patch (*Gaeumannomyces graminis*). Therefore, sustaining creeping bentgrass at consistently high quality requires a preventive fungicide program during the growing season as well as during the over-wintering period for snow mold. Voids in the turf caused by these diseases can allow weeds such as annual bluegrass to invade creeping bentgrass turfs. Because these same diseases can be serious on fairways, preventive fungicide treatment is essential to sustaining disease-free creeping bentgrass fairway turf.

Insect Control

On greens, black cutworms may occur regularly and should be treated as soon as the initial evidence of feeding becomes apparent. Otherwise, insecticides should be used only when potentially serious injury occurs or is anticipated.

PERENNIAL RYEGRASS

Perennial ryegrass (*Lolium perenne* L.) is a cool-season species adapted primarily to temperate climates as a perennial turfgrass. It does best in sunny locations with moist neutral to slightly acid soils with moderate to high fertility. As it tolerates moderate mowing heights, perennial ryegrass can be used for tees, fairways, and roughs. Its growth habit is bunch-type and it tends to form clumpy turfs unless interseeded to reestablish plant density where disease or injury has caused thinning. Because of rapid seed germination and vigorous seedling growth, a new perennial ryegrass turf can be established and form a playable surface very quickly.

Mowing

Perennial ryegrass fairways should be mowed within a range of ½ to ⅞ in. (13 to 22 mm) three to four times per week, with clippings returned or preferably removed. Closer mowing might be tolerated by some cultivars but would reduce this species ability to compete with annual bluegrass. Special precautions should be taken to avoid scalping, as this creates ports of entry for annual bluegrass from seed germination and reduces the resistance of perennial ryegrass to the expansion of existing annual bluegrass populations from vegetative growth.

Because of the rapid vertical shoot growth of perennial ryegrass during cool weather, a mowing frequency of three to four times per week is usually required. PGRs, including trinexapac ethyl (Primo), may be used to reduce vertical shoot growth and thus mowing frequency. Clipping removal may improve appearance and would remove annual bluegrass seed heads but is not as important as it is for creeping bentgrass fairways. It is usually practiced after rains have delayed mowing, and clipping yields would be unusually high.

Fertilization

Nitrogen fertilization of perennial ryegrass fairways usually ranges from 0.3 to 0.7 lb N per 1000 ft² (0.15 to 0.35 kg per 100 m²) per growing month. The low end of the rate spectrum is used during the midsummer period, when high temperatures induce high rates of photorespiration, resulting in reduced photoassimilate production and growth. N fertilization should also be reduced or eliminated during the midfall period to enhance winter hardening and reduce the potential for low-temperature kill during the overwintering period.

Other primary—as well as secondary and tertiary—nutrients should be provided as part of a balanced fertility program, as suggested by soil and plant-tissue test results. Excessive use of phosphorus should be avoided, as this may favor annual bluegrass. Potassium applications in excess of recommendations based on soil tests are sometimes advocated because of the special importance that potassium has in enhancing turfgrass tolerance to environmental stress—including wear, heat, and drought stresses—during the summer months. An emerging rule of thumb is to apply potassium routinely at 75 to 100 percent of the nitrogen application rate (Beard, 2002). In summer, potassium sulfate (K_2SO_4) is preferable to potassium chloride (KCl), due to its substantially lower salt index and therefore reduced foliar burn potential. An additional benefit from the use of the sulfate carrier is the added contribution of sulfur to the fertilization program.

Soil reaction should be managed to sustain the pH within a range of 6.0 to 7.0 for optimum growth of perennial ryegrass, with sulfur or ammonium sulfate used to lower the pH and lime used to raise it to the optimum range.

Irrigation

An irrigation program should be established to sustain sufficient growth while ensuring that fairway drainage is adequate to avoid oxygen deficiencies in the root zone that might otherwise favor annual bluegrass. Where divots are seeded routinely to promote recovery, some midday syringing may be needed to encourage germination and seedling growth.

Topdressing

As perennial ryegrass is not a thatch former, topdressing is not usually practiced or necessary.

Cultivation

Core cultivation is usually restricted to the midspring and late summer/early fall periods when perennial ryegrass is not under severe heat and drought stresses. September cultivation (in the northern hemisphere) is also done to prepare a seedbed for *interseeding* operations. Since perennial ryegrass has a bunch-type growth habit, vegetative recovery from damage or disease occurs entirely from tillering, resulting in the commonly observed clumpy growth of this species. Thus, interseeding in late summer or early fall provides an *induced recuperative potential* that does not otherwise occur with this species.

Chemical Control of Annual Bluegrass

Perennial ryegrass has a high level of tolerance to ethofumesate (Prograss). Whereas the maximum rate that can be used on creeping bentgrass is 0.75 lb a.i. per acre (0.84 kg a.i. per ha), perennial ryegrass may be treated with 2 lb a.i. per acre (2.24 kg a.i. per ha). Thus, ethofumesate is the principal herbicide used for controlling annual bluegrass infestations in perennial ryegrass fairways.

Fairways are generally interseeded with perennial ryegrass in late summer. Ethofumesate is applied 1 to 2 weeks after emergence of the ryegrass when the seedlings are 1 in. (25 mm) tall or after the first mowing. A second application is typically made 21 to 28 days later. Because the efficacy of ethofumesate is enhanced by cold weather, late-season applications usually provide the greatest control of annual bluegrass.

Controlling Other Weeds

Preemergence herbicides may be used for preventing the emergence of summer annual grasses, including crabgrass and goosegrass, and an array of broadleaf weeds. These herbicides include dithiopyr (Dimension); several dinitroaniline herbicides, including benefin and trifluralin (Team), pendimethalin (Pre-M, Pendulum), and prodiamine (Barricade); and oxadiazon (Ronstar). Care must be taken to ensure that herbicide residues do not impede the development of perennial ryegrass seedlings from late-summer inter-seedings. This is a special concern with prodiamine, given its long residual activity at higher application rates.

Postemergence control of newly germinated stands of crabgrass in perennial ryegrass fairways can be obtained from applications of fenoxyprop p-ethyl (Acclaim Extra); however, its efficacy declines as crabgrass plants mature and produce more tillers. Efficacy is also reduced under droughty conditions or if fenoxyprop p-ethyl is mixed with 2,4-D and related phenoxycarboxylic acid herbicides. Well-established crabgrass (i.e., more than four tillers) is more easily controlled with postemergence applications of quinclorac (Drive). Dithiopyr is unique among the preemergence herbicides in that it also provides some early postemergence activity. Where dithiopyr is applied to untillered crabgrass or to crabgrass with no more than two tillers, satisfactory control can be achieved. A possible alternative to conventional preemergence herbicides for crabgrass control is corn gluten meal (CGM), a by-product of corn wet milling containing a series of dipeptides that inhibit mitosis in root tips.

Postemergence control of young populations of goosegrass germinating throughout the summer can obtained from applications of fenoxyprop *p*-ethyl at light rates every 2 weeks. These applications could be made in combination with fungicides where disease control is needed.

Clover, chickweed, and other broadleaf weeds can be controlled with postemergence applications selected phenoxycarboxylic acid (mecoprop, dichloroprop), pyridinecarboxylic acid (triclopyr, clopyralid), quinolinecarboxylic acid (quinclorac), benzoic acid (dicamba), and aryltriazolinone (carfentrazone) herbicides applied in combinations or, in some cases, individually.

Disease Control

Perennial ryegrass is highly susceptible to several important diseases, including: brown patch (*Rhizoctonia solani*), gray leaf spot (*Pyricularia grisea*), brown blight (*Drechslera siccans*), *Pythium* blight (*Pythium* spp.), red thread (*Laetisaria fruciformis*), crown rust (*Puccinia coronata*), and *Typhula* blight (*Typhula incarnata, T. ishikarienis*). Because of the severity of some diseases of perennial ryegrass (e.g., gray leaf spot), a preventive fungicide program may be needed during the summer months as well as during the over-wintering period for snow mold control.

Insect Control

Insecticides should be used only when potentially serious injury occurs or is anticipated.

BERMUDAGRASS

Bermudagrasses used for greens and fairways are usually sterile interspecific hybrids developed from common bermudagrass [Cynodon dactylon (L.) Pers.] and African bermudagrass (*Cynodon traansvalensis* Burtt-Davy), forming hybrid bermudagrass (*Cynodon dactylon* × *C. traansvalensis*) that must be propagated vegetatively. Naturally occurring hybrids are called *magennis bermudagrass* (*Cynodon* × *magennisii* Hurcombe). Some fairways are established from improved cultivars of common bermudagrass, some of which can be propagated from seed.

Bermudagrasses are warm-season species adapted to warm-subtropical and tropical climatic zones; however, some cold-hardy ecotypes and cultivars of *C. dactylon* persist in cool-subtropical and even warm-temperate climatic zones. Bermudagrasses are not very shade tolerant and require sunny locations, preferably with moist fertile soils of slightly acid to neutral pH. As hybrid bermudagrasses tolerate close mowing, they can be used for greens as well as for tees and fairways. With a growth habit that is both stoloniferous and rhizomatous, bermudagrasses vary widely in texture and shoot growth orientation, with some cultivars tending toward prostrate growth and others more upright.

Mowing

Greens
Bermudagrass greens should be mowed within a range of $\frac{1}{10}$ to $\frac{3}{16}$ in. (2.5 to 4.8 mm) six to seven times per week, with clippings removed. Tifgreen and Tifdwarf are turf-type hybrid bermudagrass cultivars that have been used for many years on greens; these should be mowed at $\frac{3}{16}$ in. (4.8 mm). Champion is an example of one of the new ultradwarf hybrids that tolerate mowing as low as $\frac{1}{10}$ in. (2.5 mm) and sustain shoot densities comparable to the high-density, upright-growing creeping bentgrasses.

Fairways
Bermudagrass fairways should be mowed within a range of $\frac{7}{16}$ to $\frac{5}{8}$ in. (11 to 16 mm) three to five times per week, with clippings returned.

Fertilization

Greens
Bermudagrass greens require generally higher nitrogen fertilization rates than do creeping bentgrass greens. This usually entails applying

soluble nitrogen at rates of $\frac{1}{5}$ to $\frac{1}{2}$ lb N per 1000 ft^2 (98 to 245 g N per 100 m^2) every 2 weeks during the growing season. More frequent applications, or higher rates using slowly soluble nitrogen carriers, may be needed on high sand greens where substantial nutrient leaching occurs or on intensively trafficked greens requiring more recuperative growth. However, some of the newer ultradwarf cultivars have a substantially lower nitrogen requirement for sustaining shoot density and playability than other turf-type hybrid bermudagrasses.

Nitrogen fertilization should cease 3 to 4 weeks prior to the anticipated overseeding date to minimize competition between the bermudagrass and the cool-season turfgrasses used for overseeding.

Other primary—as well as secondary and tertiary—nutrients should be provided as part of a balanced fertility program, as suggested by soil and plant-tissue test results. Among the tertiary nutrients, iron is the one most likely to be deficient, especially on very sandy or alkaline soils. Incorporating iron into fungicide sprays can correct deficiencies and produce darker green foliage. Other tertiary nutrients that may be deficient in high-sand bermudagrass greens include copper and manganese.

Soil reaction should be managed to sustain the pH within a range of 6.0 to 7.0 for optimum growth of hybrid bermudagrass, with sulfur used to lower the pH and lime used to raise it to the optimum range.

Fairways

Nitrogen is usually applied regularly throughout the growing season, except for the low-temperature hardening period just prior to winter dormancy and the spring root-decline period of several weeks just after greenup. Iron chlorosis may occur on bermudagrass fairways following spring greenup when cold temperatures limit iron uptake, as well as in midsummer where soil alkalinity limits iron uptake. Other micronutrients that may be deficient include copper and manganese on sandy, alkaline soils and molybdenum on sands. Regular use of other nutrients should be based on soil and tissue test results, as excessive use can result in zinc and copper toxicity. Soil reaction should be managed to sustain the pH within the range 6.0 to 7.0 for optimum growth of bermudagrasses, with sulfur or ammonium sulfate used to lower the pH and lime used to raise it to the optimum range.

Irrigation

Greens

Irrigation is needed to meet the moisture requirements of a bermuda-grass community; sustain adequate growth to compensate for losses due to senescence, disease, and mechanical injury; and maintain shoot density for playability. Following overseeding bermudagrass greens with cool-season turfgrasses, uniform distribution of irrigation water is essential for ensuring a uniform turfgrass stand during the overwintering period.

Topdressing

Greens

Bermudagrass greens require more topdressing than creeping bentgrass greens due to the higher rate at which thatch forms, and Tifgreen bermudagrass requires more than Tifdwarf. As with the Penn A- and G-series creeping bentgrasses, the new dwarf bermuda-grasses require even more frequent sand topdressings during the portion of the season in which they are growing actively. Topdressing bermudagrass greens every 1 to 3 weeks, depending on the specific cultivar, would require 0.2 to 0.4 yd^3 per 1000 ft^2 (0.14 to 0.28 m^3 per 100 m^2) (Beard, 2002).

Cultivation

Greens

Frequent shallow vertical mowing is an important practice for controlling grain in bermudagrass greens. The newer ultradwarf cultivars, such as Champion and Tifeagle, require frequent light brushings, as vertical mowing tends to cause injury from which these cultivars are slow to recover. Coring, followed by topdressing that is sufficient to fill the holes with fresh media, dilutes the accumulation of organic residues and improves internal drainage.

Fairways

Bermudagrass fairways should be core cultivated, with soil cores reincorporated for alleviating soil compaction and controlling thatch. Vertical mowing may also be used to aid in thatch management. The preferred timing of these operations is in the first half of the growing season to ensure that sufficient time is available for complete recovery of the turf before winter.

Fall Overseeding

Greens

Bermudagrass greens in subtropical climates are typically overseeded in the fall with cool-season turfgrasses, including perennial ryegrass (*Lolium perenne*), rough bluegrass (*Poa trivialis*), or mixtures with these as well as other turfgrass species [e.g., fine fescues (*Festuca* spp.), creeping bentgrass (*Agrostis stolonifera*)]. Through the establishment of temporary turfgrass communities during the overwintering period, color and playability are maintained or enhanced and the dormant bermudagrass is protected from traffic-induced injury. Overseeding is timed in the fall when temperatures have dropped sufficiently to slow the growth of bermudagrass, but are still favorable for rapid establishment of cool-season turfgrasses. This occurs when the daily mean soil temperature at the 4-in. (100-mm) depth is between 72 and 78°F (22 to 26°C). Above this range, bermudagrass competition and seedling diseases are serious threats to the successful establishment of cool-season turfgrasses; below this range, germination may be too low and seedling growth too slow to provide a satisfactory stand.

With season-long programs of vertical mowing and topdressing to control thatch and core cultivation to alleviate soil compaction, the number and intensity of operations employed to prepare a bermudagrass green for overseeding can be reduced; however, careful and timely preparations are needed to ensure successful establishment of the overseeded turfgrasses. These operations may include the following steps:

- *Step 1*: Core cultivate 4 to 6 weeks prior to overseeding to alleviate compaction and allow the holes to close, thus preventing a speckled growth pattern from the overseeded turfgrasses.

- *Step 2*: Withhold nitrogen fertilization to minimize competition from the bermudagrass, but fertilize with phosphorus and potassium in accordance with soil test results to provide nutrients for promoting root growth of overseeded turf-grasses, 3 to 4 weeks prior to overseeding.

- *Step 3*: Vertical mow in several directions to open the turf, followed by close mowing to remove all debris, and topdress with approximately 0.5 yd^3 per 1000 ft^2 (0.35 m^3 per 100 m^2) to provide a smooth seedbed, 10 to 14 days prior to overseeding to allow the slits to recuperate.

- *Step 4*: Refrain from mowing 2 or 3 days prior to overseeding or raise the mowing height to about ¼ in. (6.4 mm) 1 week prior to overseeding to stabilize the seed from washing on sloping sites. An additional operation that might be included is the application of the PGR trinexapac-ethyl (Primo) 1 to 5 days prior to overseeding to further reduce competition from bermudagrass, especially where post-seeding warm weather occurs that might stimulate bermudagrass growth. With intensive vertical mowing as part of Step 3, however, the benefits realized from the use of a PGR may be quite minimal.

There is currently a debate over the advisability of overseeding greens of the new ultradwarf bermudagrasses. Because of the density of these cultivars, more cultivation is usually required, causing more injury, from which they are slow to recover. Where overseeding is not practiced, mowing heights should be raised to ¼ in. (6.4 mm) to protect the crowns from excessive wear.

The overseeding operation involves applying seed uniformly over the site at the proper seeding rate, drag matting the seed into the turf, lightly topdressing again, and drag matting to work the top-dressing soil into the turf. Then initiate a frequent irrigation program to maintain a moist seedbed and promote favorable germination and seedling development. Following seedling emergence, preventive fungicides should be used to provide protection from *Pythium* root rot (*Pythum* spp.) and *Rhizoctonia* brown patch (*Rhizoctonia solani*) diseases. Initial mowing is higher than normal, perhaps up to ½ inch (13 mm) for perennial ryegrass, to allow the seedlings to develop properly and begin tillering, then reduced in ¹⁄₁₆-in. (1.5-mm) increments until a ³⁄₁₆-in. (4.8-mm) mowing height is reached. These early mowings should be conducted with sharp reel blades and bedknives, and when the grass is dry, to minimize seedling injury. Fertilization should be withheld for at least 3 weeks to avoid stimulating the bermudagrass, then performed at 2- to 3-week intervals to provide ¼ to ½ lb N per 1000 ft^2 (123 to 245 g N per 100 m^2) with each application, using a soluble nitrogen source. These applications should be supplemented with phosphorus, potassium, manganese, and iron to sustain healthy growth of the cool-season turfgrasses. A preventive fungicide program, if followed, provides an additional measure of protection from dollar spot (*Rutstroemia floccosum*) and other diseases.

Seeding rates vary with the species used for overseeding. On greens, perennial ryegrass is seeded at 25 to 40 lb per 1000 ft^2 (12 to 20 kg per 100 m^2), rough bluegrass at 8 to 12 lb per 1000 ft^2 (4 to 6 kg per 100 m^2), mixtures of 75 percent perennial ryegrass and 25 percent rough bluegrass or 25 percent Chewings fescue at 30 to 40 lb per 1000 ft^2 (15 to 20 kg per 100 m^2), and mixtures of 80 percent Chewings fescue and 20 percent rough bluegrass at 20 to 25 lb per 1000 ft^2 (10 to 12 kg per 100 m^2). Seed used for overseeding bermudagrass greens should be treated with fungicides to reduce the potential for seedling disease development.

In spring, the green undergoes a "transition" back to bermudagrass, as increasing temperatures stress the cool-season turfgrass community while stimulating a resurgence of bermudagrass growth. Some of the more heat-tolerant perennial ryegrasses are slow to succumb to heat stress, delaying transition and threatening the survival of bermudagrass. To facilitate spring transition, the following measures may be implemented when nighttime soil temperatures at the 4-in. (100-mm) depth reach 62°F (17°C): reduce mowing height to ⅛ to ⁵⁄₁₆ in. (3.2 to 4.0 mm), then adjust to the height for sustaining the bermudagrass through the summer; fertilize with soluble nitrogen at 1.2 lb N per 1000 ft^2 (245 g N per 100 m^2); and begin a weekly schedule of shallow vertical mowing.

One of the consequences of overseeding bermudagrass greens is increased pressure for annual bluegrass invasion, which is largely a reflection of the cultural practices associated with planting and maintaining overseeded cool-season turfgrasses.

Fairways

In addition to providing a green playing surface and better traffic tolerance during the overwintering period, bermudagrass fairways may be overseeded to mark more clearly the location of the desired landing areas for golfers. They are not prepared as extensively for overseeding as are greens. The process usually begins with close mowing and removal of debris to open the turf and allow seed to reach the soil surface. To the extent that thatch exists, core cultivation, with the soil cores reincorporated, should be performed several weeks prior to overseeding. Where the thatch layer is too deep to be completely modified with soil from reincorporation of cores, some vertical mowing may be needed to remove a portion of the thatch and open up the remainder to facilitate soil core reincorporation from subsequent core cultivation.

Seeding rates vary with the species used for overseeding; however, these are usually at one-fourth the rate used for greens. For example, perennial (or annual or intermediate) ryegrass is seeded at 6 to 10 lb per 1000 ft^2 (3 to 5 kg per 100 m^2).

Chemical Control of Annual Bluegrass

Greens

Pronamide (Kerb) is a preemergence herbicide that should be applied at least 60 days prior to overseeding (usually, late July or early August in the northern hemisphere); otherwise, herbicide residues could impede successful establishment of overseeded cool-season turfgrasses. For those wishing to overseed prior to the 60-day waiting period, activated charcoal may be applied at 2 to 4 lb per 1000 ft^2 (1 to 2 kg per 100 m^2) at least 7 days prior to overseeding to adsorb and thus deactivate the pronamide residue.

Other preemergence herbicides, including bensulide (Bensumec, Pre-San) and dithiopyr (Dimension), may be used on bermudagrass greens for annual bluegrass control; however, there are several restrictions on the use of these herbicides. Bensulide provides variable control of annual bluegrass and the ryegrass tolerance range is narrow, requiring at least 4 months between its application and ryegrass overseeding. Although effective for controlling annual bluegrass and some crabgrasses, dithiopyr should not be used on Tifgreen bermudagrass. At least 8 weeks is required between dithiopyr application and overseeding with cool-season turfgrasses; a second application should be made in early winter for year-round control of these species.

Fenarimol (Rubigan) is a systemic fungicide that can also provide preemergence and some early postemergence control of the annual biotype of annual bluegrass without adversely affecting bermudagrass or perennial ryegrass. For strictly preemergence control, two (6 oz per 1000 ft^2, 1.9 g per 100 m^2) or three (4 oz per 1000 ft^2, 1.3 g per 100 m^2) sequential applications of the 1AS formulation should be made 10 to 14 days apart, with the last application completed 14 days prior to overseeding perennial ryegrass. Where some annual bluegrass escapes are evident, a follow-up application at 2 to 4 oz per 1000 ft^2 (0.7 to 1.3 g per 100 m^2) should be made in early winter; later applications will be ineffective, as fenarimol's postemergence activity on annual bluegrass is limited to new seedlings. Where rough bluegrass or creeping bentgrass is used for overseeding, no postemergence applications should be made, and the last preemergence application should be no later than 30 days prior to overseeding. Fenarimol is currently regarded as the standard product for preemergence control of annual bluegrass in bermudagrass greens, despite the fact that it is no longer labeled for this use.

Fairways

In addition to the products discussed for controlling annual bluegrass in bermudagrass greens, several others may be used for bermudagrass fairways. Ethofumesate (Progras) is used for preemergence and postemergence control of annual bluegrass in dormant bermudagrass fairways overseeded with perennial ryegrass. Rough bluegrass and fine fescues are very sensitive to ethofumesate and are likely to be damaged from its use. Its first application is made 30 to 45 days after overseeding, but only if the bermudagrass is completely dormant; otherwise, serious injury can occur. A second application may be made 30 days later, but not after mid January in the northern hemisphere, as this may cause injury or delayed greenup in the spring.

Bensulide (Bensumec, Pre-San) applied 120 days prior to overseeding can provide preemergence control of annual bluegrass while allowing an acceptable stand of perennial ryegrass to be established. The preemergence herbicides dithiopyr (Dimension) and benefin

(Balan) may also be used, with waiting periods of 56 and 45 days, respectively, before overseeding is conducted.

Controlling Other Weeds

Greens

In addition to their role in controlling annual bluegrass during periods of seed germination, preemergence herbicides can be used for preventing the emergence of summer annual grasses, including crabgrass and goosegrass, and an array of broadleaf weeds. These herbicides include bensulide (Bensumec, Pre-San, Weedgrass Preventer), bensulide and oxadiazon (Goosegrass/Crabgrass Control), dithiopyr (Dimension), napropamide (Devrinol), pendimethalin (Pre-M, Pendulum), and prodiamine (Barricade).

Postemergence control of newly germinated stands of crabgrass in creeping bentgrass fairways can be obtained from applications of fenoxyprop p-ethyl (Acclaim Extra); however, its efficacy declines as crabgrass plants mature and produce more tillers. Well-established crabgrass (i.e., more than four tillers) is more easily controlled with postemergence applications of quinclorac (Drive). While postemergence control of young populations of goosegrass germinating throughout the summer can be obtained from applications of fenoxyprop p-ethyl at light rates every 2 weeks, diclofop-methyl (Illoxan) is often effective with a single application, especially on young goosegrass. Neither fenoxyprop p-ethyl nor diclofop-methyl should be mixed with 2,4-D or related phenoxycarboxylic acid herbicides, as they may reduce efficacy or increase phytotoxicity.

Broadleaf weeds can be controlled with postemergence applications of selected phenoxycarboxylic acid (mecoprop, dichloroprop), pyridinecarboxylic acid (triclopyr, clopyralid), quinolinecarboxylic-acid (quinclorac), benzoic acid (dicamba), and aryltriazolinone (carfentrazone) herbicides applied in combinations or, in some cases, individually.

Fairways

The list of preemergence herbicides that can also be used for preventing the emergence of summer annual grasses and broadleaf weeds in bermudagrass fairways is larger than that for greens because of the greater tolerance of fairway turf to these materials. This list includes benefin (Balan) alone or with oryzalin (XL) or trifluralin (Team), bensulide (Bensumec, Pre-San, Weedgrass Preventer) alone or with oxadiazon (Goosegrass/Crabgrass Control), dithiopyr (Dimension), napropamide (Devrinol), oryzalin (Surflan), oxadiazon (Ronstar), pendimethalin (Pre-M, Pendulum), and prodiamine (Barricade).

Disease Control

Bermudagrasses are highly susceptible to several important diseases, including bermudagrass decline (*Gaeumannomyces graminis*), dollar spot (*Rutstroemia floccosum*), leaf blotch (*Bipolaris cynodontis*), bermudagrass rust (*Puccinia cynodontis*), and spring dead spot (many species). Although higher-cut bermudagrass turfs can be sustained with little or no fungicide use, greens require a preventive fungicide program for controlling diseases during the growing season in humid regions and a curative program in arid and semiarid regions.

Insect Control

Insecticides should be used only when potentially serious injury occurs or is anticipated.

APPENDIX 1

Herbicides Used on Annual Bluegrass Turfs

Common Name	Trade name	Class	Formulations	Manufacturer	Signal Word
Atrazine	Atrazine 4L	s-triazines	4 L	UHS	Caution
	Atrazine 90 WDG		90 WDG	UHS	Caution
Benefin	Balan 2.5G	Dinitroanalines	2.5% G	UHS	Caution
Benefin and trifluralin	Team Pro 0.86%	Dinitroanalines	0.86G fertilizer	Dow AgroSciences	Caution
	Team Pro with fertilizer		0.86G fertilizer	LESCO	Caution
	Team 2G		2% G	LESCO	Caution
	Team 2G		2% G	UHC	Caution
Bensulide	Bensumec 4LF	Phosphorodithioates	4 lb/gal LF	PBI/Gordon	Caution
	Pre-San 12.5G		12.5% G	PBI/Gordon	Warning
	Pre-San 17G		7% G	PBI/Gordon	Warning
Bentazon	Lescogran	Benzothiadiazinones	4 lb/gal SC	LESCO	Caution
	Basagran T/O		4 lb/gal SL	TopPro	Caution
Bispyribac	Velocity	Pyrimidiny benzoates	2 lb/gal SC	Valent USA	Caution
Carfentrazone[a]	Many	Aryltriazolinone	Many	PBI/Gordon	Caution
Chlorsulfuron	Corsair	Sulfonylureas	75 WDG	Riverdale	Caution
Clopyralid[b]	Lontrel	Pyridinecarboxylic acids	40.9% SC	Dow AgroSciences	Caution

Herbicides Used on Annual Bluegrass Turfs

Common Name	Trade name	Class	Formulations	Manufacturer	Signal Word
2,4-D[b]	Many	Phenoxycarboxylic acids	Many	Many	Danger
Dazomet	Basamid Granular	Thiadiazine	99 G	BASF	Warning
Dicamba[b]	Many	Benzoic acids	Many	Many	Caution
Dichloroprop[b]	Many	Phenoxycarboxylic acids	Many	Many	Caution
Dithiopyr	Dimension 0.10% plus fertilizer	Pyridines	0.10% G fertilizer	LESCO	Caution
	Dimension 0.15% plus 13-2-5		0.15% G fertilizer	LESCO	Caution
	Dimension		1 lb/gal EC	Rohm & Haas	Caution
	Dimension Ultra WSP		40% WSP	Rohm & Haas	Caution
Ethofumisate	Prograss EC	Penzofuranes	1.5 lb/gal EC	Aventis	Danger
Fenoxyprop p-ethyl	Acclaim Extra	Aryloxyphenoxy-propionates	0.57 EC	Aventis	Caution
Glufosinate-ammonium	Finale	Phosphinic acids	1 lb/gal SC	Aventis	Warning
Glyphosate	GlyphoMate	Glycines	4 lb/gal SC	PBI/Gordon	Caution
	Prosecutor		4 lb/gal SC	LESCO	Caution
	Roundup PRO		4 lb/gal SC	Monsanto	Caution
	Razor		4 lb/gal SC	Riverdale	Caution
Halosulfuron	Manage	Sulfonylureas	75 WDG	Monsanto	Caution
Imazaquin	Image 70DG	Imidazolinones	70 DG	BASF	Caution
Mecoprop[b]	Many	Phenoxycarboxylic acids	Many	Many	Caution
Metolachlor	Pennant	Chloroacetamides	8 lb/gal EC	Syngenta	Caution
Metribuzin	Sencor 75 Turf Herbicide	a-triazines	75 DF	Bayer	Caution
Oryzalin	Surflan A.S.	Dinitroanalines	4 lb/gal EC	Dow AgroSciences	Caution
Oxadiazon	Ronstar 50WSP	Oxidiazoles	50 WSP	Bayer	Warning
	Ronstar 0.95% + 20-2-20 fertilizer		0.95% G fertilizer	LESCO	Warning

Herbicides Used on Annual Bluegrass Turfs

Common Name	Trade name	Class	Formulations	Manufacturer	Signal Word
Oxadiazon (*cont.*)	Ronstar 0.95% + 5-10-15 mini fertilizer		0.95% G fertilizer	LESCO	Warning
	Ronstar G		2 G	Bayer	Warning
Pendimethalin	Pendulum 2G	Dinitroanalines	2 G	BASF	Caution
	Pendulum 3.3EC		3.3 EC	BASF	Caution
	Pendulum 75DF		60 WDG	BASF	Caution
	Pre-M 0.86% plus fertilizer		0.86% G fertilizer	LESCO	Caution
	Pre-M 3.3EC		3.3 lb/gal EC	LESCO	Caution
Prodiamine	Barricade 65WG	Dinitroanalines	65% WG	Syngenta	Caution
Pronamide	Kerb WSP	Benzamides	51% WSP	Rohm & Haas	Caution
Quinclorac	Drive 75DF	Quinolinecarboxylic acids	75 DF	BASF	Caution
Rimsulfuron	TranXit GTA	Sulfonylureas	25 DF	Griffin	Caution
Siduron	Tupersan	Ureas	50 WP	PBI/Gordon	Caution
Simazine	Princep	s-triazines	4 lb/gal F	Syngenta	Caution
Triclopyr[b]	Turflon Ester	Pyridinecarboxylic acids	61.6 % EC	Dow AgroSciences	Danger
Triclopry and clopyralid	Confront	Pyridinecarboxylic acids	EC 12.1% clopyralid and 33% triclopyr	Dow AgroSciences	Danger

[a] A new herbicide that is used in combinations with 2,4-D, mecoprop, and dicamba for broad-spectrum control of broadleaf weeds.

[b] These herbicides are often included in two-, three-, and four-way combinations for broad-spectrum control of broadleaf weed species.

APPENDIX 2

Fungicides Used on Annual Bluegrass Turfs

Common Name	Trade Name	Class	Formulation	Manufacturer	Signal Word
Azoxystrobin	Heritage	Methoxy-acetylate, Qol	50 WP	Syngenta	Caution
Chloroneb	Teremec	Chlorophenyl	65 WP	PBI/Gordon	Caution
Chlorothalonil	Daconil 2787	Nitrite	4.17 F	Syngenta	Warning
	Daconil Ultrex		82.5 WDG	Syngenta	Danger
	Daconil Weather Stik		6 F	Syngenta	Warning
	Manicure 6 Flowable		6 F	LESCO	Warning
	Manicure Ultrex Turf Care		82.5 WDG	LESCO	Danger
Etridiazole	Koban 1.3 G	Triadiazole	1.3 G	The Andersons	Caution
	Koban 30		30% liquid	The Andersons	Warning
	Terrazole		35 WP	Uniroyal	Warning
Fenarimol	Patchwork	Pyrimidine	0.78 G	Riverdale	Caution
	Rubigan A.S.		11.6 EC	Gowan	Caution
Flutolanil	Prostar 70 WP	Benzamide	70 WP	Agrevo	Caution
Fosetyl-Al	Chipco Signature	Phosphonates	80 WP	Bayer	Caution
	Prodigy 80 DG		80 DG	LESCO	Caution
Iprodione	Chipco 26GT Flo	Dicarboximide	2 F	Bayer	Caution

Fungicides Used on Annual Bluegrass Turfs

Common Name	Trade Name	Class	Formulation	Manufacturer	Signal Word
Mancozeb	Flowable Mancozeb 4	Carbamate	4 F	LESCO	Caution
	Fore		80 WP	Rohm & Haas	Caution
	Fore Flowable		4 F	Rohm & Haas	Caution
	Fore FloXL		4 F	Rohm & Haas	Caution
	Mancozeb DG		75 DG	LESCO	Caution
	Protect T/O		80 WSB	Cleary	Caution
Mefenoxam	Subdue MAXX	Acylalanine	21.3% F	Novartis	Caution
	Subdue GR		0.97% G	Novartis	Caution
Myclobutanil	Eagle	Tridiazole	40WS	Rohm & Haas	Caution
Pentachloronitro -benzene (PCNB)	Defend 10G	Chlorinated hydrocarbon	10 G	Cleary	Caution
	Defend 4[F]		4 F	Cleary	Caution
	Engage 10G		10 G	UHS	Caution
	PCNB 12.5% plus fertilizer		12.5 G	LESCO	Caution
	Revere 4000 Flowable Fungicide		4 F	LESCO	Caution
	Revere WSP		75 WSP	LESCO	Caution
	Terraclor		75 WP	Uniroyal	Caution
	Terraclor 400		4 F	Uniroyal	Caution
	Turfcide 10% Granular		10 G	Uniroyal	Caution
Propiconazol	Banner GL	Triadiazole	41.8 WSP	Novartis	Warning
	Banner MAXX		14.3% EC	Novartis	Warning
Propamacarb	Banol	Carbamate	6 E	Bayer	Caution
Thiophanate-M	3336 F	Benzimidazoles	4.5 F	Cleary	Caution
	3336 G		2.08 G	Cleary	Caution
	3336 WSP		50 WSP	Cleary	Warning
	Cavalier 2G		2.08 G	LESCO	Caution
	Cavalier 4.5F		4.5 F	LESCO	Caution

Fungicides Used on Annual Bluegrass Turfs

Common Name	Trade Name	Class	Formulation	Manufacturer	Signal Word
Thiophanate-M (*cont.*)	Cavalier 50 WSB		50 WSB	LESCO	Caution
	Fungo Flo		4.5 F	The Andersons	Caution
	Fungo 50 WSB		50 WSB	The Andersons	Caution
	Systemic Fungicide		2.3 G	The Andersons	Caution
	Systec 1998 Flowable		4.5 F	Regal Chemical	Caution
	Systec 1998 WDG		85 WDG	Regal Chemical	Caution
Triadimefon	Accost 1G	Triadiazole	1 G	UHS	Caution
	Bayleton 25		25 WSP	Bayer	Caution
	Bayleton 50		50 WSP	Bayer	Caution
	Granular Turf Fungicide		1 G	LESCO	Caution
	Strike 25 WDG		25 WDG	Olympic	Caution
Trifluxzstrobin	Compass O	Methoxy-acetylate, Qo1	50 WDG	Bayer	Caution
Vinclozolin	Curalan		4.17 F	BASF	Caution
	Curalan DF		50 DF	BASF	Caution
	Curalan EG		50 WDG	BASF	Caution
	Vorlan DF		50 DF	The Andersons	Caution
	Touche Flowable		4.17 F	LESCO	Caution
	Touche EG		50 WDG	LESCO	Caution

APPENDIX 3
Insecticides Used on Annual Bluegrass Turfs

Common Name	Trade Name	Class	Formulation	Manufacturer	Signal Word
Acephate	Orthene Turf, Tree & Ornamental Spray	Organophosphate	75 WP	Valent	Caution
	Pinpoint		15 G	Valent	Caution
Azadirachtin	Azatin XL	Insect growth regulator	0.265 lb/gal	Olympic	Caution
Bacillus thuringiensis kurstaki (Bt)	Biobit	Bacteria	14.5 BIU/lb	Abbott	Caution
	Dipel 2X		14.5 BIU/lb	Abbott	Caution
	Dipel DF		14.5 BIU/lb	Abbott	Caution
	Mattch		14.5 BIU/lb	Mycogen	Caution
	MVP II		14.5 BIU/lb	Mycogen	Caution
Bendiocarb	Turcam	Carbamate	76 WP	Bayer	Warning
	Turcam 2.5 G		2.5 G	Bayer	Warning
Bifenthrin	Talstar Lawn & Tree Flowable	Synthetic pyrethroid	0.66 ib/gal	FMC	Caution
	Talstar GC Granular		0.2 G	FMC	Caution
	Talstar GC Granular		0.66 lb/gal	FMC/Whitmire	Caution
	Talstar Nursery Flowable		0.66 lb/gal	FMC	Caution

Insecticides Used on Annual Bluegrass Turfs

Common Name	Trade Name	Class	Formulation	Manufacturer	Signal Word
Carbaryl	8% Sevin Granular Carbaryl Insecticide	Carbamate	8 G	The Andersons	Caution
	Fertilizer with Sevin		6.2 G	The Andersons	Caution
	Sevin 4% with fertilizer		4 G	LESCO	Caution
	6.3% Sevin brand Granular Carbaryl Insecticide		6.3 G	LESCO	Caution
	Sevin brand SL		4 lb a.i./gal	LESCO	Caution
	Chipco Sevin brand 80 WSP		80 WSP	Bayer	Warning
	Chipco Sevin brand SL		4 lb a.i./gal	Bayer	Caution
	Sevin 10 G		10 G	United Hort Supply	Caution
Chlorpyrifos	2.32% Dursban	Organophosphate	2.32 G	The Andersons	Caution
	0.97% Dursban		0.97 G	The Andersons	Caution
	0.5% Dursban		0.5 G	The Andersons	Caution
	Fertilizer with Dursban (various)		0.92/0.65/ 0.57 G	The Andersons	Caution
	Dursban 50 W WSP		50 WSP	Dow AgroSciences	Warning
	Dursban Pro		2 lb a.i./gal	Dow AgroSciences	Caution
	Professional Pest Control Dursban 0.5 G		0.5 G	LESCO	Caution
	Dursban 0.74% plus fertilizer		0.74 G	LESCO	Caution
	Dursban 0.97% plus fertilizer		0.97 G	LESCO	Caution
	1% Dursban		1 G	LESCO	Caution
	2.32 Granular Insecticide		2.32 G	LESCO	Caution
	Insecticide III		1.34 G	Scotts	Caution
	Turf fertilizer plus Insecticide		0.65 G	Scotts	Caution

Insecticides Used on Annual Bluegrass Turfs

Common Name	Trade Name	Class	Formulation	Manufacturer	Signal Word
Chlorpyrifos (*cont.*)	Dursban 2 Coated Granules		2 G	United Hort Supply	Warning
	Dursban TNP		4 lb a.i./gal	United Hort Supply	Warning
Cyflutherin	Tempo 20 WP	Synthetic pyrethroid	20 WP	Bayer	Caution
	Tempo 20 WP		2 lb a.i./gal	Bayer	Warning
	Tempo 20 WP (Golf Course WSP)		20 WP	Bayer	Caution
	Tempo 20 WP (Power Pak)		20 WP	Bayer	Caution
Deltamethrin	DeltaGard GC	Synthetic pyrethroid	5 SC	Bayer	Caution
	DeltaGard T & O		0.1 G	Bayer	Caution
	DeltaGard T & O 5 SC		5 SC	Bayer	Caution
	DeltaGard GC Granular		0.1 g	Bayer	Caution
Diazinon	5% Diazinon	Organophosphate	5 G	The Andersons	Caution
	Fertilizer with 3.33 Diazinon		3.33 G	The Andersons	Caution
	Diazinon		3.33 G	LESCO	Caution
	Diazinon AG 600		4.67 lb a.i./gal	LESCO	Caution
	Diazinon 4 E		4 lb a.i./gal	Terra	Caution
	Diazinon		5 G	United Hort Supply	Caution
Ethoprop	Chipco Mocap brand 10G GC	Organophosphate	10 G	Aventis	Warning
Halfenozide	Mach 2 Granular	Insect growth regulator	1.5 G	Rohmid	Caution
	Mach 2 Liquid		2 lb a.i./gal	Rohmid	Caution
Imidacloprid	Fertilizer with Merit Insecticide	Neonicotinold	0.2 G	The Andersons	Caution
	Merit 0.5 G		0.5 G	Bayer	Caution
	Merit 75 WP		75 WP	Bayer	Caution

Insecticides Used on Annual Bluegrass Turfs

Common Name	Trade Name	Class	Formulation	Manufacturer	Signal Word
Imidacloprid (*cont.*)	Merit 75 WSP		75 WSP	Bayer	Caution
	Lebanon Fertilizer with Merit 0.3% Insecticide		0.3 G	Lebanon	Caution
	Merit 0.2 plus fertilizer		0.2 G	LESCO	Caution
	Turf Fertilizer plus Merit Insecticide		0.2 G	Scotts	Caution
Isofenphos	Oftanol 1.5%	Organophosphate	1.5 G	The Andersons	Caution
	Fertilizer with Oftanol		1.5 G	The Andersons	Caution
	Oftanol 2		2 lb a.i./gal	Bayer	Warning
	Oftanol 1/5% and fertilizer		1.5 g	LESCO	Caution
	Oftanol 1.5%		1.5 g	LESCO	Caution
Lambda-cyhalothrin	Battle CS	Synthetic pyrethroid	0.88 lb a.i./gal	LESCO	Caution
	Battle GC		0.88 lb a.i./gal	LESCO	Caution
	Battle WP		10 WP	LESCO	Warning
	Scimitar CS		0.88 lb a.i./gal	Syngenta	Caution
	Scimitar GC		0.88 lb a.i./gal	Syngenta	Caution
	Scimitar WP		10 WP	Syngenta	Warning
Permethrin	Astro	Synthetic pyrethroid	3.2 lb a.i./gal	FMC	Caution
Soap	M-Pede	Insecticidal soap	49% a.i.	Mycogen	Warning
Spinosad	Conserve SC	Actinomycete-fermentation derived	1 lb a.i./gal	Dow AgroSciences	Caution
Trichlorfon	Dylox 6.2 G	Organophosphate	6.2 G	The Andersons	Caution
	Dylox 6.2 G		6.2 G	Bayer	Caution
	Dylox 80 T&O		80 WP	Bayer	Warning

REFERENCES

Adams, W. A. 1980. Effects of nitrogen fertilization and cutting height on the shoot growth, nutrient removal and turfgrass composition of an initially perennial ryegrass dominant sports turf. In J. B. Beard (ed.) *Proceedings of the 3rd International Turfgrass Conference,* Munich, Germany, July 11–13, 1977. International Turfgrass Society, ASA, CSSA, and SSSA, Madison, WI, pp. 343–350.

Allard, R. W., S. K. Jain, and P. L. Workman. 1968. The genetics of inbreeding populations. *Advances in Genetics* 14:55–131.

Allen, P. S., D. B. White, and A. H. Markhart. 1993. Germination of perennial ryegrass and annual bluegrass seeds subjected to hydration–dehydration cycles. *Crop Science* 33:1020–1025.

Beard, J. B. 1964. Effects of ice, snow and winter covers on Kentucky bluegrass, annual bluegrass and creeping bentgrass. *Crop Science* 4:638–640.

Beard, J. B. 1966. Direct low temperature injury of nineteen turfgrasses. *Quarterly Bulletin of the Michigan Agricultural Experiment Station* 48(3):377–383.

Beard, J. B. 1970. An ecological study of annual bluegrass. *USGA Green Section Record* 8(2):13–18.

Beard, J. B. 1973. *Turfgrass: Science and Culture.* Prentice-Hall, Englewood Cliffs, New Jersey.

Beard, J. B. 2002. *Turf Management for Golf Courses*, 2nd ed. Ann Arbor Press, Chelsea, MI.

Beard, J. B., and D. P. Martin. 1970. Influence of water temperature on submersion tolerance of four grasses. *Agronomy Journal* 62:257–259.

Beard, J. B., P. E. Rieke, A. J. Turgeon, and J. M. Vargas, Jr. 1978. Annual bluegrass (*Poa annua* L.): description, adaptation, culture and control, *Agricultural Experiment Station Research Report*. Michigan State University, East Lansing, MI.

Begon, M., J. L. Harper, and C. R. Townsend. 1986. *Ecology, Individuals, Populations and Communities*. Blackwell, Oxford.

Bell, G. E., E. Odorizzi, and T. K. Danneberger, 1997. Controlling annual bluegrass and rough bluegrass in creeping bentgrass fairways: a nutritional approach. *Agronomy Abstracts* 89:122.

Bewley, J. D. and M. Black. 1994. *Seeds: Physiology of Development and Germination*, 2nd ed. Plenum Press, New York, p. 232.

Blackman, P. A., P. J. Landschoot, and D. R. Huff. 1999. Variation in pathogenicity, morphology and RAPD markers profiles in *Colletotrichum graminicola* from turfgrass. *Crop Science* 39:1129–1135.

Bogart, J. E. 1972. Factors influencing competition of annual bluegrass (*Poa annua* L.) within established turfgrass communities. M. S. thesis. Michigan State University, East Lansing, MI.

Brede, A. D. 1982. Interaction of three turfgrass species. Ph. D. dissertation. Pennsylvania State University, University Park, PA (Dissertation Abstracts 82–28866).

Burpee, L. L., L. M. Kaye, L. G. Goulty, and M. B. Lawton. 1987. Suppression of gray snow mold on creeping bentgrass by an isolate of *Typhula phacorrhiza*. *Plant Disease* 71: 97–100.

Carrow, R. N., and A. M. Petrovic. 1992. Effects of traffic on turfgrasses. In D. V. Waddington, R. N. Carrow, and R. C. Shearman (eds.), *Turfgrass*. Agronomy Monograph 32. ASA, CSSA, and SSSA, Madison, WI.

Chapman, G. P. and W. E. Peat. 1992. *An Introduction to the Grasses*. CAB International, Wallingford, Berkshire, England.

Cockerham, S. T. and J. W. Whitworth. 1967. Germination and control of annual bluegrass. *Golf Superintendent* 35(5):14,17,45–46.

Connell, J. H. 1990. Apparent versus real competition in plants. In J. B. Grace and D. Tilman,(eds.), *Perspectives on Plant Competition,* Academic Press, New York.

Cordukes, W. E. 1977. Growth habit and heat tolerance of a collection of *Poa annua* plants. *Canadian Journal of Plant Science* 57:1201–1204.

Danneberger, T. K. 1993. *Turfgrass Ecology and Management*. G. I. E, Inc. Publishers, Cleveland, OH.

Danneberger, T. K., and J. M. Vargas, Jr. 1984. Annual bluegrass seedhead emergence as predicted by degree-day accumulation. *Agronomy Journal* 76:756–758.

Danneberger, T. K., J. M. Vargas, Jr., P. E. Rieke, and J. R. Street. 1983. Anthracnose development on annual bluegrass in response to nitrogen carriers and fungicide application. *Agronomy Journal* 75:35–38.

Danneberger, T. K., J. M. Vargas, Jr., and A. L. Jones. 1984. A model for weather-based forecasting of anthracnose on annual bluegrass. *Phytopathology* 74:448–451.

Danneberger, T. K., B. E. Branham, and J. M. Vargas Jr. 1987. Mefluidide applications for annual bluegrass seedhead suppression based on degree–day accumulation. *Agronomy Journal* 79:69–71.

Danneberger, T. K., M. J. Carroll, J. M. Vargas, Jr., and P. E. Rieke. 1995. Susceptibility of *Poa annua* L. to anthracnose as influenced by water stress. *Journal of Turfgrass Management* 1:19–24.

Darmency, H., and J. Gasquez. 1983. Esterase polymorphism and growth form differentiation in *Poa annua* L. *New Phytologist* 95:289–297.

Darmency, H., A. Berti, J. Gasquez, and A. Matejicek. 1992. Association of esterase isoenzymes with morphology in F_2 progenies of two growth variants in *Poa annua* L. *New Phytologist* 121(4):657–661.

Dernoeden, P. H. 2000. *Creeping Bentgrass Management: Summer Stresses, Weeds and Selected Maladies*. Ann Arbor Press, Chelsea, MI.

Dest, W. M., and D. W. Allinson. 1981. Influence of nitrogen and phosphorus fertilization on the growth and development of *Poa annua* L. (annual bluegrass). In R. W. Sheard (ed.) *Proceedings of the 4th International Turfgrass Research Conference*, Guelph, Ontario, Canada. July 19–23, 1981. International Turfgrass Research Society and Ontario Agricultural College, University of Guelph, Guelph, Ontario, Canada, pp. 325–332.

Diesburg, K. L., and N. E. Christians. 1989. Seasonal application of ethephon, flurprimidol, mefluidide, paclobutrazol and amidachlor as they affect Kentucky bluegrass shoot morphogenesis. *Crop Science* 29:841–847.

Dionne, J., P. A. Dube, M. Lunganirre, and Y. Desjardins.1999. Golf green soil and crown-level temperatures under winter protection covers. *Agronomy Journal* 91:227–233.

Ellis, W. M. 1973. The breeding system and variation on populations of *Poa annua* L. *Evolution* 27:656–662.

Engel, R. E. 1967. Temperatures required for germination of annual bluegrass and colonial bentgrass. *Golf Superintendent* 35(9):20, 23.

Escritt, J. R., and D. C. Legg. 1970. Fertilizer trials at Bingley.In *Proceedings of the First International Turfgrass Research Conference,* Harrogate, England, July 15–18, 1969. Sports Turf Research Institute, Bingley, Yorkshire, England, pp. 185–190.

Ferguson, N. L. 1936. A greenskeeper's guide to the grasses: the meadowgrasses. *Journal of the Board of Greenkeeping Research* 4(15):274–279.

Firbank, L. G. and A. R. Watkinson. 1990. On the effects of competition: from monocultures to mixtures. In J. B. Grace and D. Tilman (eds.) *Perspectives on Plant Competition*. Academic Press, New York.

Gaussoin, R. E. 1988. Species dominance in mixed stands of creeping bentgrass and annual bluegrass: I. Influence of cultural factors on annual bluegrass/creeping bentgrass interference. Ph.D. dissertation. Michigan State University, East Lansing, MI.

Gibeault, V. A. 1971. Perenniality of *Poa annua* L. Ph.D. dissertation. Oregon State University, Corvallis, OR.

Gibeault, V. A. 1974. *Poa annua. California Turfgrass Culture* 24:13–16

Gibeault, V. A. and N. R. Goetze. 1973. Annual meadowgrass. *Journal of the Sports Turf Research Institute* 48:9–19.

Gleason, H. A. 1968. *The New Britton and Brown Illustrated Flora of the Northeastern United States and Adjacent Canada*. New York Botanical Garden, Hafner Publishing, New York.

Glinski, J., and J. Lipiec. 1990. *Soil Physical Conditions and Plant Roots*. CRC Press, Boca Raton, FL.

Golembieski, R. C., J. M. Vargas, Jr., A. L. Jones, and A. R. Detweiler. 1995. Detection of demethylation inhibiting (DMI) resistance in *Sclerotinia homoeocarpa* populations. *Plant Disease* 79:491–493.

Goodman, D. M., and L. L. Burpee. 1991. Biological control of dollar spot of creeping bentgrass. *Phytopathology* 81:1438–1446.

Goss, R. L. 1964. The ecology of *Poa annua*, annual bluegrass. *Proceedings of the 18th Annual Northwest Turfgrass Conference*. pp. 6–11.

Goss, R. L., S. E. Brauen, and S. P. Orton. 1975. The effects of N, P, K and S on *Poa annua* L. in bentgrass putting green turf. *Journal of the Sports Turf Research Institute* 51:74–82.

Grace, J. B. 1990. On the relationship between plant traits and competitive ability. In J. B. Grace and D. Tilman (eds.), *Perspectives on Plant Competition,* Academic Press, New York.

Grime, J. P. 1977. Evidence for the existence of three primary strategies in plants and its relevance to ecological and evolutionary theory. *American Naturalist* 111:1169–1194.

GRIN. 1996. *National Genetic Resources Program,* ARS, USDA. http://www. ars–grin. gov/cgi–bin/npgs/html/taxon. pl?405224.

Hamilton, G. W. 2001. Environmental factors affecting creeping bentgrass and annual bluegrass tolerance to ice coverage. Ph.D. dissertation. Pennsylvania State University, University Park, PA.

Harivandi. M. A., J. D. Butler, and L. Wu. 1992. Salinity and turfgrass culture. In D. V. Waddington, R. N. Carrow, and R. C. Shearman (eds.), *Turfgrass.* Agronomy Monograph 32. ASA, CSSA, and SSSA. Madison, WI.

Horvath, B. J. 1999. Comparison of *Colletotrichum graminicola* spp. causing crown rotting anthracnose to *Colletotrichum graminicola* and *Colletotrichum sublineolum* isolates using isozyme markers. M. S. thesis. Michigan State University, East Lansing, MI.

Hovin, A. W. 1957a. Germination of annual bluegrass seed. *Southern California Turf Culture* 7(2):13.

Hovin, A. W. 1957b. Variations in annual bluegrass. *Golf Course Reporter* 25(9): 18–19.

Hovin, A. W. 1958a. Meiotic chromosome pairing in amphihaploid *Poa annua* L. *American Journal of Botany* 45:131.

Hovin, A. W. 1958b. Reduction of self–pollination by high night temperature in naturally self–fertilized *Poa annua*. *Agronomy Journal* 50:369.

Hubbard, C. E. 1959. *Grasses*. Penguin, Baltimore, MD.

Huff, D. R. 1998. The case for *Poa annua* on golf course greens. *Golf Course Management* 66(9):54–56.

Huff, D. R. 1999. For richer, for *Poa*: cultivar development of greens–type *Poa annua*. *USGA Green Section Record* 37(1):11–14.

Johnson, P. G. 1991. Factors affecting the seed set in *Poa annua* L. using an excised stem technique. M. S. thesis. University of Minnesota, St. Paul, MN.

Johnson, P. G., and D. B. White. 1997a. Flowering responses of selected annual bluegrass genotypes under different photoperiods and cold treatments. *Crop Science* 37:1543–1547.

Johnson, P. G., and D. B. White. 1997b. Vernalization requirements among selected genotypes of annual bluegrass (*Poa annua* L.). *Crop Science* 37:1538–1542.

Johnson, P. G. and D. B. White. 1998. Inheritance of flowering pattern among four annual bluegrass (*Poa annua* L.) genotypes. *Crop Science* 38:163–168.

Johnson, P. G., B. A. Ruemmele, P. Velguth, D. B. White, and P. D. Ascher. 1993. An overview of *Poa annua* reproductive biology. *International Turfgrass Society Research Journal* 7:798–804, R. N. Carrow, N. E. Christians, and R. C. Shearman (eds.). Intertec Publishing, Overland Park, KS.

Juhren, M., W. Noble, and F. W. Went. 1957. The standardization of *Poa annua* as an indicator of smog concentrations: I. Effects of temperature, photoperiod, and light intensity during growth of test plants. *Plant Physiology* 32:576–586.

Juska, F. V., and A. A. Hanson. 1969. Nutritional requirements of *Poa annua* L. *Agronomy Journal* 61:466–468.

Koshy, T. K. 1968. Evolutionary origin of *Poa annua* L. in the light of karyotypic studies. *Canadian Journal of Genetic Cytology* 10:112–118.

Koshy, T. K. 1969. Breeding systems in annual bluegrass, *Poa annua* L. *Crop Science* 9:40–43.

Kosky, A. J. 1983. Seasonal rooting characteristics of five cool season turfgrasses. M. S. thesis. Ohio State University, Columbus, OH.

Law, R. 1979. The cost of reproduction in annual meadowgrass. *American Naturalist* 113(1):3–16.

Law, R. 1981. The dynamics of a colonizing population of *Poa annua*. *Ecology* 62: 1267–1277.

Law, R., A. D. Bradshaw, and P. D. Putwain. 1977. Life history variation in *Poa annua*. *Evolution* 31:233–246.

Lewis, B. 1994. *Genes V*. Oxford University Press, Oxford.

Lush, W. M. 1988a. Biology of *Poa annua* in a temperate zone golf putting green (*Agrostis stolonifera/Poa annua*): I. The above ground population. *Journal of Applied Ecology* 25:977–988.

Lush, W. M. 1988b. Biology of *Poa annua* in a temperate zone golf putting green (*Agrostis stolonifera/Poa annua*): I. The seed bank. *Journal of Applied Ecology* 25:989–997.

Lush, W. M. 1989. Adaptation and differentiation of golf course populations of annual bluegrass (*Poa annua*). *Weed Science* 37:54–59.

Lush, W. M. 1990. Turf growth and performance evaluation based on turf biomass and tiller density. *Agronomy Journal* 82:505–511.

Madden, E. A. 1967. *Poa annua*: problem weed in New Zealand. *Golf Superintendent* 35(1):13–14.

Mitra, S., and T. E. Vrabel. 2000. Biologically based weed control strategies for *Poa annua* management using *Xanthomonas campestris* pv. *Poanna*. *Pro-*

ceedings of the 54th Annual Meeting of the Northeastern Weed Science Society 54:67.

Nannfeldt, J. A. 1937. The chromosome numbers of *Poa*, sect. *Ochlopoa* A and Gr. and their taxonomic significance. *Botaniska Notiser* 1937:238–257.

Neidlinger, T. J. 1965. *Poa annua* L.: Susceptibility to several herbicides and temperature requirements for germination. M.S. thesis, Oregon State University, Corvallis, OR, pp. 1–97.

Nelson, E. B., and C. M. Craft. 1991. Introduction and establishment of strains of *Enterobacter cloacae* in golf course turf for biological control of dollar spot. *Plant Disease* 75:510–514.

Niemczyk, H. D., and D. M. Dunbar. 1976. field observations, chemical control, and contact toxicity experiments on *Ataenius spretulus,* a grub pest of turf grass. *Journal of Economic Entomology* 69:345–348.

Peel, C. H. 1982. A review of the biology of *Poa annua* L. with special reference to sports turf. *Journal of the Sports Turf Research Institute* 58:28–40.

Potter, D. A. 1998. Destructive Turfgrass Insects: Biology, Diagnosis and Control. Ann Arbor Press, Chelsea, MI.

Ruemmele, B. A. 1989. Reproductive biology of *Poa annua* L. Ph.D. dissertation. University of Minnesota, Duluth, MN.

Sartain, J. B. 1985. Effects of acidity and N source on the growth and thatch accumulation of 'Tifgreen' bermudagrass and on soil nutrient retention. *Agronomy Journal* 77:33–36.

Sarukhan, J. 1974. Studies on plant demography: *Ranunculus repens* L., *R. bulbosus* L. and *R. acris* L.: II Reproductive strategies and seed population dynamics. *Journal of Ecology* 62(1):151–177.

Sears, M. K. 1979. Damage to golf course fairways by *Aphodius granaries* (L.) (Coleoptera: Scarabaeidae). *Proceedings of the Entomological Society of Ontario* 109:48.

Smitely, D., and T. Davis. 1999. Causes of black turfgrass ataenius and aphodus outbreaks on the golf course: pesticides use may increase ataenius numbers by reducing predator populations. *Golf Course Management* 67: 53–55.

Sprague, H. B. and G. W. Burton. 1937. Annual bluegrass (*Poa annua* L.) and its requirements for growth. *New Jersey Agricultural Experiment Station Bulletin 630.*

Stebbins, G. L. 1950. *Variation and Evolution in Plants.* Columbia University Press, New York.

Street, J. R., P. R. Henderlong, R. J. Cooper, and K. J. Karnok. 1984. The effect of mefluidide on annual bluegrass (*Poa annua* L.) quality and rooting. *Agronomy Abstracts,* p. 149.

Sweeney, P. M., and T. K. Danneberger. 1995. RAPD characterization of *Poa annua* L. populations in golf course greens and fairways. *Crop Science* 35:1676–1680.

Sweeney, P. M., and T. K. Danneberger. 1997. Annual bluegrass segregation on greens and fairways. *Golf Course Management* 65(4):49–52.

Tashiro, H. 1987. *Turfgrass Insects of the United States and Canada.* Cornell University Press, Ithaca, NY.

Tashiro, H., C. L. Murdoch, R. W. Straub, and P. J. Vittum. 1977. Evaluation of insecticides on *Hyperodes* sp., a pest of annual bluegrass turf. *Journal of Economic Entomology* 70:729–733.

Tilman, D. 1990. Mechanisms of plant competition for nutrients: the elements of a predictive theory of competition. In J. B. Grace and D. Tilman (eds.), *Perspectives on Plant Competition,* Academic Press, New York.

Timm, G. 1965. Biology and systematics of *Poa annua. Feitschrift fuer Acker- und Pflanzenbau* 122:267–294.

Turgeon, A. J. 2002a. Competition between *Agrostis stolonifera* and *Poa annua* populations in turfgrass communities. *Science and Golf* IV:643–647.

Turgeon, A. J. 2002b. *Turfgrass Management,* 6th ed. Prentice-Hall, Upper Saddle River, NJ.

Turgeon, A. J., and J. M. Vargas, Jr. 1979. An approach to turfgrass cultivar evaluation. In J. B. Beard (ed.), *Proceedings of the 3rd International Turfgrass Research Conference.* American Society of Agronomy, Madison, WI, pp. 19–30.

Tutin, T. G. 1952. Origin of *Poa annua. Nature* 169:160.

Tutin, T. G. 1957. A contribution to the experimental taxonomy of *Poa annua* L. *Watsonia* 4:1–10.

Van Arendonk, J. J. C.M., and H. Poorter. 1994. The chemical composition and anatomical structure of leaves of grass species differing in relative growth rate. *Plant, Cell, and Environment* 17: 963–970

Van Wijk, A. L. M., W. B. Verhaegh, and J. Beuving. 1977. Grass sportsfields: top layer compaction and soil aeration. *Rasen Turf Gazon* 8:47–52.

Vargas, J. M. 1976. Disease poses threat to annual bluegrass. *Golf Course Superintendent* 44:42–45.

Vargas, J. M., Jr. 1981. *Management of Turfgrass Diseases.* Burgess, Minneapolis, MN, p. 204.

Vargas., J. M., Jr. 1994. *Management of Turfgrass Diseases,* 2nd ed. Lewis/CRC Press. Boca Raton, FL.

Waddington, D. V., and T. L. Zimmerman. 1972. Growth and chemical composition of eight grasses grown under high water table conditions. *Communications in Soil Science and Plant Analysis* 3:329–337.

Waddington, D. V., T. R. Turner, J. M. Duich, and E. L. Moberg. 1978. Effect of fertilization on 'Penncross' creeping bentgrass. *Agronomy Journal* 70:713–718.

Warwick, S. I. 1979. The biology of Canadian weeds: 37. *Poa annua* L. *Canadian Journal of Plant Science* 59(4):1053–1066.

Watschke, T. L., and R. E. Schmidt. 1992. Ecological aspects of turf communities. In D. V. Waddington, R. N. Carrow, and R. C. Shearman (eds.), *Turfgrass.* Agronomy Monograph 32. ASA, CSSA, and SSSA, Madison, WI.

Watson, L. ,and M. J. Dallwitz. 1992. *The Grass Genera of the World.* CAB International, Wallingford, Berkshire, England.

Wegner, G. S., and H. D. Niemczyk. 1981. Bionomics and phenology of *Ataenius spretulus*. *Annals of the Entomological Society of America* 74:374–384.

Wehner, D. J., and T. L. Watschke. 1981. Heat tolerance of Kentucky bluegrasses, perennial ryegrasses, and annual bluegrass. *Agronomy Journal* 73:79–84.

Wells, G. J. 1974. The biology of *Poa annua* and its significance in grassland. *Herbage Abstracts* 44:385–391.

Wells, G. J. 1975. The autoecology of *Poa annua* L. in perennial ryegrass pastures. *Journal of the Australian Institute of Agricultural Sciences* 41:51–54.

Wilkinson, J. F., and D. T. Duff. 1972. Rooting of *Poa annua* L., *Poa pratensis* L. and *Agrostis palustris* Huds. at three soil bulk densities. *Agronomy Journal* 64:66–68

Wu, L., and A. Harivandi. 1993. Annual bluegrass ecology and management. *Golf Course Management* 61(3):100, 102, 104, 106.

Wu, L., I. Till-Bottraud, and A. Torres. 1987. Genetic differentiation in temperature-enforced seed dormancy among golf course populations of *Poa annua* L. *New Phytologist* 107:623–631.

Xu, X., and C. F. Mancino. 2001. Iron pumps up creeping bentgrass. *Golf Course Management* 69(2): 49–51.

Youngner, V. G. 1959. Ecological studies on *Poa annua* in turfgrasses. *Journal of the British Grassland Society* 14(4):233–247.

INDEX

A

Acclaim Extra. *See* fenoxyprop *p*-ethy
Accost 1G. *See* triadimefon
acephate, 143
acervuli, 72
acid-forming fertilizer, 24
adaptability of annual bluegrass, 48
Agrostis ipsilon (Hufnagel). *See* black
    cutworm
Agrostis stolonifera L. *See* creeping
    bentgrass
aleurone layer, 21
algae, 78, 89–90
Allard, R. W., 35
alleles, 36
allelopathic interaction, 43
Allen, P. S., 22
Allinson, D. W., 44
allotetraploids, 8
alpigena Schur, 6
amidochlor, 59
ammonium sulfate, 24, 105
anastomosis, 18
anatomy, 16–20
annual biotypes, 4–5, 7
annual bluegrass
    genetics of, 7–10
    popularity of, 2
    taxonomy, 3–7
annual bluegrass weevil, 97–98, 99, I–8
annual grasses, 64–66
anthracnose, 2, 71–73, 78
ants, 99
aphodius grubs, 90–94, 99
aquatica Aschers, 6
aryltriazolinone herbicides, 68, 118, 132
asperites, 17
Astro. *See* permethrin
ataenius grubs, 90–91, I–6

atrazine, 135
auricles, 12
autotetraploids, 7–8
azadirachtin, 99, 100, 143
Azatin XL. *See* azadirachtin
azoxystrobin, 73, 75, 78, 81, 87, 139

B

Bacillus thuringiensis, 99, 143
bacterial wilt. *See Xanthomonas campestris*
Balan. *See* benefin
Balan 2. 5G. *See* benefin
Banner. *See* propiconazol
Banol. *See* propamocarb
Barricade. *See* prodiamine
Basagran. *See* bentazon
Basagran T/O. *See* bentazon
Basamid Granular. *See* dazomet
Battle. *See* lambda-cyhalothrin
Bayleton. *See* triadimefon
Beard, J. B., 22, 61
bendiocarb, 92, 99, 143
benefin, 114, 118, 122, 133, 135
bensulide, 130, 131, 133, 135
Bensumec 4LF. *See* bensulide
bentazon, 68, 69, 135
benzimidazole, 73, 84, 86
benzoic acid herbicides, 68, 118, 132
bermudagrass, 123–33
    chemical control of annual bluegrass
      among, 130–32
    controlling other weeds, 132–33
    cultivating, 126–27
    disease control, 133
    fall overseeding, 127–30
    fertilizing, 124–26
    insect control, 133
    mowing, 124
    topdressing, 126

bifenthrin, 99, 143

Biobit. *See bacillus thuringiensis*

biotypes of bluegrass, 4–7

birds, 94

bispyribac, 112, 115, 135

black cutworm, 98–100, I–8

black layer formation, 105

Blackman, P. A., 72

black turfgrass aphodius grubs, 90–94, 99

black turfgrass ataenius, 90–92, 99, I–6

blade, 12

bluegrass, Kentucky, 39, 40, 45–46, 115

Bogart, J. E., 22

bracteata, 5

Briggs, 33

broadleaf weeds, 68–71, 118, 132

brown patch, 78, 79–81, I–4, I–5

bulliform cells, 16

Burpee, L. L., 14, 28, 77, 86

C

carbaryl, 92, 97, 99, 144

carbohydrate production, 39

carfentrazone, 69, 132, 135

caryopsis, 20

Casparian strip, 18

Cavalier. *See* thiophanate-m

Cerastium vulgatum L. *See* mouse-ear
    chickweed

CGM (corn gluten meal), 65, 69, 118, 123

C. graminicola, 72

Champion bermudagrass, 124, 126

charcoal, 130

chemical control of annual bluegrass
   within bermudagrass, 130–32
   within creeping bentgrass, 112–16

chickweed, 118

Chipco 26GT Flo. *See* iprodione

Chipco Mocap brand 10G GC. *See*
    ethoprop

Chipco Sevin. *See* carbaryl

Chipco Signature. *See* fosetyl-aluminum

chloroneb, 78, 83, 139

chlorothalonil, 78, 80, 81, 84, 86, 87, 90,
    139

chlorpyrifos, 92, 99, 144, 145

chlorsulfuron, 135

chromosones. *See* genetics

Class A plant growth regulators, 58

Class B plant growth regulators, 58–59

Class C plant growth regulators, 59

Class D plant growth regulators, 59–60

Class E plant growth regulators, 60–62

cleistoamy, 34

clipping removal, 104, 120

clopyralid, 68, 69, 132, 135

clover, 118

Cockerham, S. T., 22, 23

cold, effect of, 61–62

coleoptile, 21–22

coleorhiza, 21

collar, 12

Colletotrichum graminicola. See
    anthracnose

Compass O. *See* trifluxystrobin

competition, 41–46
   community-based (interspecific)
     competition, 43–46
   overview, 41
   population-based (intraspecific)
     competition, 41–43

Confront. *See* triclopyr

Conserve SC. *See* spinosad

continual types, 33

control of annual bluegrass. *See*
    bermudagrass; creeping bentgrass;
    perennial ryegrass

copper, 89, 125

Cordukes, W. E., 28–29

core cultivation, 54–55
   bermudagrass, 126–27
   creeping bentgrass, 110–11

corn gluten meal (CGM), 65, 69, 118, 123

Corsair. *See* chlorsulfuron

cortex cells, 18

cottony blight. *See Pythium* blight

covers, 62

crabgrass
   in annual bluegrass, 64–65, 69, I–1
   in bermudagrass, 132
   in creeping bentgrass, 117, 118
   in perennial ryegrass, 122–23

Craft, C. M., 77

creeping bentgrass, 102–19
   biological control of, 116–17

creeping bentgrass (*cont.*)
    chemical control of, 69, 112–16
    controlling other weeds, 117–18
    cultivating, 109–11
    disease control, 119
    fertilizing, 104–6
    insect control, 119
    irrigating, 106–7
    mowing, 102–4
    photos of, I–3, I–4
    rolling, 111–12
    seasonal growth of, 40, 45–46
    topdressing, 107–9
cross-pollination, 33–34
crown, 13
crown rotting anthracnose (CRA), 72–73,
    I–3
crows, 91, 94
cultivar selection, 49
cultivation, 54–56
    bermudagrass, 126–27
    creeping bentgrass, 109–11
    drill cultivation, 111
    hollow-tine cultivation (HTC), 54,
        110–11
    perennial ryegrass, 121
    water-injection cultivation, 111
    See also core cultivation
cultural requirements, 47–100
    controlling winter injury, 60–62
    diseases, 71–90
        algae, 89–90
        anthracnose, 71–73
        bacterial wilt, 88–89
        fairy rings, 87
        See also patch diseases; snow molds
    establishment, 49
    insects, 90–100
        annual bluegrass weevil, 97–98
        aphodius grubs, 93–94
        black cutworm, 98–100
        black turfgrass ataenius, 91–92
        Japanese beetle, 94–97
        white grubs, 90–91
    overview, 48
    pest management, 63–71
        annual grasses, 64–66
        broadleaf weeds, 68–71

        perennial grasses and sedges, 66–68
        weeds, 63–64
    primary cultural operations, 50–53
    supplementary cultural operations,
        54–62
        cultivation, 54–56
        plant growth regulators (PGRs),
        56–60
        rolling, 56
Curalan. *See* vinclozolin
cuticles, 17
Cutless plant growth regulator, 57
cutworms, 98–100
cyanobacteria, 89
cycling, 23
cyflutherin, 145
cyfluthrin, 99
Cynodon magennis Hurcombe. *See*
    magennis bermudagrass
Cyperus esculentus L. *See* yellow nutsedge

D

Daconil. *See* chlorothalonil
Danneberger, T. K., 32, 36, 59, 71
Darmency, H., 34, 35
Davis,, 93
dazomet, 116, 136
Dd/dd genes, 36
decortication, 27
decumbens Nolte ex Junge, 6
Defend. *See* pentachloronitro-benzene
    (PCNB)
DeltaGard. *See* deltamethrin
deltamethrin, 99, 145
demethylation inhibitors, 73
Dest, W. M., 44
Devrinol. *See* napropamide
dew removal, 76–77
diazinon, 145
dicamba, 69, 132, 136
dicarboximide, 84, 86
dichloroprop, 69, 132, 136
diclofop-methyl, 132
Digitaria sp. *See* crabgrass
dihaploid annual bluegrass, 7–10
Dimension. *See* dithiopyr; siduron
dinitroaniline herbicides, 114, 122
Dipel. *See bacillus thuringiensis*

direct interference, 43
discoloration, 59
diseases, 71–90
  algae, 89–90
  among bermudagrass, 133
  among creeping bentgrass, 119
  anthracnose, 71–73
  bacterial wilt, 88–89
  fairy rings, 87
  See also patch diseases; snow molds
dithiopyr, 65, 66, 69, 136
  use with bermudagrass, 130–31, 133
  use with creeping bentgrass, 114
DNA. *See* genetics
dollar spot, 75–79, I–4
dormancy, 24, 37, 38
double fertilization, 29
drill cultivation, 111
Drive. *See* quinclorac
drought, 2–3
Duff, D. T., 28
Dunbar, D. M., 91
Dursban. *See* chlorpyrifos
Dylox. *See* trichlorfon

E
Eagle. *See* myclobutanil
Eco Soil Systems. *See* XPoM bioherbicide
Eleusine indica (L.) Gaern. *See* goosegrass
Ellis, W. M., 34
Embark 2S plant growth regulator, 57
Embark T&O plant growth regulator, 57
embryo, 21
endosperm, 21, 29
Engage 10G. *See* pentachloronitro-
    benzene (PCNB)
Engel, R. E., 22
Enterobacter cloacae, 77
enzymes, 21
epidermal cells, 17, 19
ethazole, 83
ethephon, 57, 60
ethofumesate, 57, 60, 136
  use with bermudagrass, 131
  use with creeping bentgrass, 114–15
  use with perennial ryegrass, 122
ethoprop, 99, 145

etridiazole, 78, 139
excelsior mats, 62

F
fairways
  bermudagrass
    cultivation, 126–27
    fall overseeding, 129–30
    mowing, 124
    weed control, 132–33
  controlling goosegrass on, 66
  controlling weeds on, 69
  creeping bentgrass
    chemical control of annual
        bluegrass, 113–17
    controlling weeds on, 117–18
    irrigating, 106–7
    mowing, 103–4
    rolling, 111–12
    topdressing, 109
  mowing, 50
  nitrogen fertilization, 51–52
fairy rings, 78, 87
fall overseeding, 127–30
fenarimol, 78, 86, 131, 139
fenoxyprop *p*-ethyl, 65, 66, 69, 118, 123,
    132, 136
Ferguson, N. L., 24
fertilization, 29, 51–52
  acid-forming fertilizer, 24
  of bermudagrass, 124–26, 128–29
  of creeping bentgrass, 104–6
  double, 29
  of perennial ryegrass, 120–21
  See also nitrogen fertilization
Finale. *See* glufosinate-ammonium
Fitzpatrick (syn. *butleri* subrm.), 81
flavescens Hausm., 5
Flowable Mancozeb 4. *See* mancozeb
flowering periods, 31–33
flurprimidol, 57, 58
flutolanil, 78, 81, 87, 139
foliar anthracnose, 71–72, I–3
Fore. *See* mancozeb
fosetyl-aluminum, 78, 83, 139
freezing conditions, 61–62
fungicides, 73, 74, 78, 81, 83

copper fungicides, 89
   use on bermudagrass, 128–29, 131
   See also names of specific fungicides
Fungo. *See* thiophanate-m
Fusarium heterosporum, 77

G

gametes for dormancy/nondormancy, 37, 38
Gasquez, J., 34
gene flow, 36
genetics, 7–10
germination and seedling development, 20–24
gibberellic acid, 57, 58, 60, 113, 115
gibberellin biosynthesis, 57
Gibeault, V. A., 4, 15–16
Gleason, H. A., 31
glufosinate-ammonium, 66, 69, 113, 136
glyphosate, 57, 59–60, 66, 69, 136
Goetze, N. R., 4
Goodman, D. M., 77
goosegrass, 65–66, 69
   in annual bluegrass, I–1
   in bermudagrass, 132
   in creeping bentgrass, 117, 118
   ideal conditions for, 63
   in perennial ryegrass, 122, 123
grain, removing from green, 55–56
Granular Turf Fungicide. *See* triadimefon
gray snow mold, 78, 85–86, I–5
grease spot. *See Pythium* blight
greens
   bermudagrass
      chemical control of annual bluegrass, 130–31
      cultivating, 126
      fall overseeding, 127–29
      mowing, 124, 124–25
      weed control, 132
   controlling weeds on, 69
   creeping bentgrass
      chemical control of annual bluegrass, 112–13
      cultivating, 109–11
      fertilizing, 104–5
      irrigating, 106

      mowing, 102–3
      topdressing, 107–9
      weed control, 117
   mowing, 50
growing-degree-days, 59
grubs, 90–94, 99, I–6
guttation fluid, 76, 77

H

halfenozide, 97, 99, 145
halosulfuron, 68, 69, 136
Harivandi, M. A., 23
heat. *See* temperature
herbicides, 59–60
   phytotoxicity from, 112
   use with bermudagrass, 130–33
   use with creeping bentgrass
      on fairways, 114–15, 117–18
      on greens, 112–13
   use with perennial ryegrass, 122
Heritage. *See* azoxystrobin
hollow-tine cultivation (HTC), 54, 110–11
Hovin, A. W., 4, 8, 14, 22
Hubbard, C. E., 31
Huff, D. R., 9–10, 26–27
hydothodes, 77
hydrolytic enzymes, 21
Hyperodes Sp. *See* annual bluegrass weevil
hypoxic, 61

I

ice-related damage, 61–62
Image 70DG. *See* imazaquin
imazaquin, 136
imidacloprid, 97, 99, 145–46
inbreeding coefficient (F), 35
inflorescence development, 29–38
   fertilization, 29
   flowering periods, 31–33
   gamete distribution for dormancy/ nondormancy, 37, 38
   phases of, 29–30
   pollination, 33–37
   seedhead production, 31–33
Insecticide III. *See* chlorpyrifos

insects, 90–100
    annual bluegrass weevil, 97–98
    aphodius grubs, 93–94
    in bermudagrass, 133
    black cutworm, 98–100
    black turfgrass ataenius, 91–92
    in creeping bentgrass, 119
    insecticides for various types, 99
    Japanese beetle, 94–97
    white grubs, 90–91
    See also pest management
intercalary meristem, 25
interseeding, 121
interspecific competition, 43–46
intraspecific competition, 41–43
iprodione, 78, 81, 87, 139
iron, 106, 125, 129
irrigation, 52–53
    bermudagrass, 126
    creeping bentgrass, 106–7
    perennial ryegrass, 121
isofenphos, 99, 146

J
Japanese beetle, 91, 94–97, 99, I–7
Johnson, P. G., 31, 32, 33, 34, 35
Juhren, M., 32

K
Kentucky bluegrass, 39, 40, 45–46, 115
Kerb WSP. *See* pronamide
Korban. *See* etridiazole
Koshy, A. J., 33

L
lambda-cyhalothrin, 99, 146
latisquama Lindm., 5
Law, R., 31
lead arsenic, 48
leaf blade, 12
leaf primordia, 25
leaf sheath, 12
Lebanon Fertilizer with Merit 0. 3%
    Insecticide. *See* imidacloprid
lemma, 20, 29
Leptosphaeria korrae J. C. Walker & A.
    M. Sm, 74–75

Lescogran. *See* bentazon
light
    effect on germination, 24
    red, 42
lime, 105
Listronotus maculicollis (Dietz). *See*
    annual bluegrass weevil
lodicules, 29
Lolium perenne L. *See* perennial ryegrass
longiglumis Lindm., 5
Lontrel. *See* clopyralid
low-temperature induction, 30
Lush, W. M., 22, 23–24, 25, 26, 31

M
macerrima Nakai ex Jansen & Wachter, 5
Mach 2 Granbular. *See* halfenozide
Mach 2 Liquid. *See* halfenozide
magennis bermudagrass, 124
Magnathae poae Landschoot & Jackson,
    73–74
magnesium, 106, 125, 129
maleic hydrazide, 59
Manage. *See* halosulfuron
mancozeb, 78, 80–81, 84, 90, 140
maneb, 80–81
Manicure 6 Flowable. *See* chlorothalonil
Manicure Ultrex Turf Care. *See*
    chlorothalonil
masked chafers, 91
mat, 108
Mattch. *See bacillus thuringiensis*
MCPA, 69
mecoprop, 69, 132, 136
mefenoxam, 140
mefenozam, 78
mefluidide, 57, 59, I–1
meristematic cells, 27
Merit. *See* imidacloprid
mesophyll cells, 17
metalaxyl, 83
methyl isocyanate (MITC) gas, 116
Metolachlor, 136
metribuzin, 136
Microdochium patch. *See* pink snow mold
midrib, 16
minima Schur, 6

MITC (methyl isocyanate) gas, 116
moisture, 22–24, 44
moles, 94
morphology, 12–16
moss, 70–71, I–2
mouse-ear chickweed, 63, 69, 70, I–2
mowing, 50
    bermudagrass, 124, 128
    creeping bentgrass, 102–4
    perennial ryegrass, 120
M-Pede. *See* soap
MVP II. *See* *Bacillus thuringiensis*
myclobutanil, 78, 140

N
Nannfeldt, J. A., 8
napropamide, 133
necrotic ring spot, 74–75, 78
Neem, 100
Neidlinger, T. J., 22
Nelsen, E. B., 77
nematodes, 96, 100
nepalensis Griseb., 6
Niemczyk, H. D., 91
nitrogen fertilization, 51–52, 65, 74
    of bermudagrass, 125, 127–28
    and brown patch, 80
    of creeping bentgrass, 104, 105, 113,
        116–17
    and Necrotic ring spot, 75
    of perennial ryegrass, 120
    and *Pythium* blight, 83
nondormancy, 37, 38
Nostoc spp., 89
nutlets, 67

O
Oftanol. *See* isofenphos
Orthene Turf, Tree & Ornamental Spray.
    See acephate
oryzalin, 133, 136
Oscillatoria spp., 89
Oust plant growth regulator, 57
outcrossing, 34–35
overseeding, 127–30
oxadiazon, 114, 118, 122, 133, 136, 137
oxtetracycliine, 89

oxygen deficiency, 61, 106, 121

P
paclobutrazol, 57, 58, 113, 115–16
palea, 20, 29
parenchyma cells, 18
patch diseases, 73–83
    brown patch, 79–81
    dollar spot, 75–79
    necrotic ring spot, 74–75
    Pythium blight, 81–83
    summer patch, 73–74
    yellow patch, 81
Patchwork. *See* fenarimol
pauciflora Fiek, 5
PCNB fungicides, 78, 86
pearlwort, 69, 70, I–2
pendimethalin, 65, 66, 69, 114, 118, 122,
    133, 137
Pendulum. *See* pendimethalin
Pennant. *See* metolachlor
Penncross creeping bentgrass, 102–3,
    108, 115
Penneagle creeping bentgrass, 115
Pennlinks creeping bentgrass, 103
pentachloronitro-benzene (PCNB), 140
perennial biotypes, 4, 6–7
perennial grasses and sedges, 66–68
perennial ryegrass, 67, 69, 119–23
pericarp, 21
permethrin, 99, 146
pest management, 63–71
    annual grasses, 64–66
    broadleaf weeds, 68–71
    perennial grasses and sedges, 66–68
    weeds, 63–64
    See also insects
Petersen's creeping bluegrass, 49
PGRs (plant growth regulators), 56–60,
    113, 120
Phendulum. *See* pendimethalin
phenoxycarboxylic acid herbicides, 65,
    68, 118, 132
phloem ducts, 18, 20
pH of soil, 45
pH of soil (*cont.*)
    and bermudagrass, 124, 125

and creeping bentgrass, 105, 106
effect on germination, 24
and perennial ryegrass, 121
Phormidium spp., 89
phosphorus, 52, 62, 105, 120, 129
photoperiodism, 32, 45
photorespiration, 39, 120
physiology, 11–46
  anatomy, 16–20
  competition, 41–46
    community-based (interspecific)
      competition, 43–46
    overview, 41
    population-based (intraspecific)
      competition, 41–43
  germination and seedling
    development, 20–24
  inflorescence development, 29–38
    fertilization, 29
    flowering periods, 31–33
    gamete distribution for
      dormancy/nondormancy, 37, 38
    phases of, 29–30
    pollination, 33–37
    seedhead production, 31–33
  morphology, 12–16
  overview, 12
  root growth, 27–29
  seasonal growth and development,
    38–40
  shoot growth, 25–27
phytochrome, 42
phytohormones, 42–43
phytotoxicity, 63, 112, I–2
picta Beck, 5
pink snow mold, 78, 83–84, I–5
Pinpoint. *See* acephate
pistil, 29
plant growth regulators (PGRs), 56–60,
    113, 120
plasticity, 35
plastochrons, 25
Poa annua. See annual bluegrass
Poa annua f. *reptans*, 49
Poa infirma H. B. K., 8, 9
Poa reptens, 49
Poa trivialis L. *See* rough bluegrass
pollination, 29, 33–37

Poorter, H., 17–18
Popillia japonica Newman. *See* Japanese
    beetle
popularity of annual bluegrass, 2
population-based (intraspecific)
    competition, 41–43
potassium, 52, 62, 105, 120–21, 129
Potter, D. A., 96
Pre-M. *See* pendimethalin
Pre-San 12. 5G. *See* bensulide
Pre-San 17G. *See* bensulide
primers, 36
Primo. *See* trinexapac-ethyl
Primo Maxx plant growth regulator, 57
Primo plant growth regulator, 57
primordia, leaf, 25
Princep. *See* simazine
prodiamine, 114, 118, 122, 133, 137
Prodigy 80 DG. *See* fosetyl-aluminum
Professional Pest Control Dursban 0. 5
    G. *See* chlorpyrifos
Prograss. *See* ethofumesate
Prograss EC. *See* ethofumesate
pronamide, 137
propagation, 49
propamocarb, 83, 140
propiconazole, 78, 86, 140
Prosecutor. *See* glyphosate
Prostar 70 WP. *See* flutolanil
Protect T/O. *See* mancozeb
Providence creeping bentgrass, 103
Proxy plant growth regulator, 57
Pseudomonas aureofaciens, 77
pseudopratensis Jansen & Wachter, 5
P. supina Schrad., 8, 9
pubescens Peterm., 5
pumila Anderss., 5
Putter creeping bentgrass, 103
pyridinecarboxylic acid herbicides, 68,
    118, 132
Pythium aphanidermatum, 84
Pythium blight, 78, 81–83, I–5
Pythium root rot, 128

Q
Qol fungicides, 73, 74, 84
quinclorac, 65, 69, 132, 137

quinolinecarboxylic acid herbicides, 68, 118, 132

R

raccoons, 94
racemosa Aschers, 5
races of bluegrass, 4
rachilla, 20, 29
radicle, 21
ramifers, 5
RAPD markers, 36–37
Razor. *See* glyphosate
red light, 42
resource competition, 43
Revere. *See* pentachloronitro-benzene (PCNB)
Rhizoctonia blight. *See* brown patch
Rhizoctonia cerealis, Van derHoeven, 81
Rhizoctonia solani Khun, 79–81
RhyzUP plant growth regulator, 57
rigidiuscula L. H. Dewey, 6
rigidly Aschers, 5
rimsulfuron, 137
rolling, 56, 111–12
Ronstar. *See* oxadiazon
root cap, 27
root growth, 27–29
roots, 14
rough bluegrass, 67, 69
roughs, mowing, 50
Roundup Pro. *See* glyphosate
Rubigan. *See* fenarimol
Ruemmele, B. A., 33
Rutstremia flocossum, Powell and Vargas, 75–76
ryegrass, perennial, 67, 69, 119–23

S

Sagina procumbens L. *See* pearlwort
Santiago Gay, 5
Sarukhan, J., 31
saturated soils, 72
scalping, 107–8
scarabs, 90–91
Scimitar. *See* lambda-cyhalothrin
sclerenchyma cells, 17
sclerotic tissue, 17

Sclerotinia homoeocarpa F. T. Bennett, 75–76
seasonal growth and development, 38–40
seasonal types, 33
seed dormancy, 24
seedhead production, 31–33
seeding. *See* overseeding
self-pollination, 33–34
Sencor 75 Turf Herbicide. *See* metribuzin
sericea Parnell, 6
Sevin. *See* carbaryl
sheath, 12
shoot growth, 25–27
sibbing, 35
siduron, 64, 65, 69, 137
sikkimensis Stapf., 6
silvatica Jansen & Wachter, 5
simazine, 137
skunks, 91, 94
SLM (specific leaf mass), 17–18
Smitely, D., 93
snow molds, 83–90
   gray snow mold, 85–86
   pink snow mold, 83–84
soap, 99, 146
sod webworms, 99
soil
   saturated soils, 72
   See also pH of soil; topdressing
solid-tine cultivation (STC), 54
specific leaf mass (SLM), 17–18
sperm nuclei, 29
spikelets, 31
spiking, 56
spinosad, 99, 146
splicing, 56
Sprague, H. B., 14, 28
STC (solid-tine cultivation), 54
Stebbins, G. L., 4
Steinernema carpocapsae, 100
stele, 18–19
stolons, 14, 25, 26
Strike 25 WDG. *See* triadimefon
Subdue. *See* mefenoxam
sulfometuron-methyl, 57, 60
sulfur, 45, 105
summer patch, 2, 73–74, 78, I–3, I–4
superficial fairy rings, 87

supplementary cultural operations,
    54–62
  cultivation, 54–56
  plant growth regulators, 56–60
  rolling, 56
Surflan A. S. *See* oryzalin
Sweeny, P. M., 36
Systec. *See* thiophanate-m
Systemic Fungicide. *See* thiophanate-m

T

Talstar GC Granular. *See* bifenthrin
Talstar Lawn & Tree Flowable. *See*
    bifenthrin
Talstar Nursery Flowable. *See* bifenthrin
taxonomy, 3–7
Team. *See* trifluralin
Team Pro. *See* benefin
tee boxes, 64
tees
  crabgrass on, 65
  goosegrass on, 66
  nitrogen fertilization, 51–52
temperature
  effect on annual bluegrass, 2–3
  effect on germination, 22–24
  effect on outcrossing, 34
  and nitrogen fertilization, 44
  and photorespiration, 39
  and seed head production, 31–32
Tempo. *See* cyfluthrin
Teremec. *See* chloroneb
Terraclor. *See* pentachloronitro-benzene
    (PCNB)
Terrazole. *See* etridiazole
tetrapolid annual bluegrass, 7–10
TGR plant growth regulator, 57
thatch patch, 87, 107–8
thinning rule, 42
thiophanate-m, 140
thiophanate-methyl, 78, 141
Tifdwarf bermudagrass, 124, 126
Tifeagle bermudagrass, 126
Tifgreen bermudagrass, 124, 126, 130
tillers, 26
Timm, G., 4, 7, 15
topdressing, 55

bermudagrass, 126
  creeping bentgrass, 107–9
  and cultivation pans, 110
  perennial ryegrass, 121
Touche. *See* vinclozolin
transpiration, 19–20
TranXit GTA. *See* rimsulfuron
triadimefon, 78, 86, 141
trichlorfon, 97, 99, 146
triclopyr, 132, 137
triflora Schur, 6
trifluralin, 114, 118, 122, 133, 135
trifluxystrobin, 78, 81, 141
Trifolium repens L. *See* white clover
Trimmer. *See* paclobutrazol
Trimmit plant growth regulator, 57
trinexapac-ethyl, 57, 58, 120, 128
tryclopyr, 68
Tupersan. *See* siduron
Turcam. *See* bendiocarb
Turfcide 10% Granular. *See*
    pentachloronitro-benzene (PCNB)
Turf Enhancer. *See* paclobutrazol
Turf fertilizer plus Insecticide. *See*
    chlorpyrifos
Turf Fertilizer plus Merit Insecticide. *See*
    imidacloprid
Turflon Ester. *See* triclopyr
Tutin, T. G., 4, 8, 14, 23, 33
Typhula blight. *See* gray snow mold
Typhula incarnata, 87
Typhula ishikariensis Imai, 85, 87
Typhula itoana Imai Lasch ex Fr., 85
Typhula phacorrhiza, 86

V

Van Arendonk, J. J., 17–18
Vargas, J. M., 2, 32, 59
variegata G. Meyer, 5
varieties of bluegrass, 3–4
vascular system, 16–20
Velocity. *See* bispyribac
vernalization, 30, 32
vertical mowing, 55–56, 128
Verti-Drain, 54
villosa Bluff and Nies, 5
vinclozolin, 78, 81, 141

viridis Lej. and Court., 5
vivipara S. F. Gray, 5
Vorlan DF. *See* vinclozolin

W
Waddington, D. V., 29
Warwick, S. I., 7, 31, 33
watering, 52–53
water-injection cultivation, 111
weed control, 63–64
   in bermudagrass, 132–33
   in creeping bentgrass, 117–18
   in perennial ryegrass, 122–23
White, D. B., 32
white clover, 63, 68–69
white grubs, 90–91
Whitworth, J. W., 22, 23
Wilkinson, J. F., 28

Winter injury, 60–62
Wu, L., 23, 24

X
Xanthomonas campestris, 60, 88–89, 117
XPoM bioherbicide (Eco Soil Systems),
   117
xylem ducts, 18

Y
yellow nutsedge, 67–68, 69
yellow patch, 78, 81
yellow tufts, 78
Younger, V. G., 4, 14–15, 22, 29

Z
Zimmerman, T. L., 29
zygote, 29